Throughout this journey we <!-- obscured by barcode -->
has surrounded me with s<!-- obscured -->
with them distinguishing details and particular characteristics. Without a doubt, Susi and Ricardo are part of those friends, and their lives manifest many beautiful details that I could easily write about, but today I'd like point out one remarkable trait they both share: the ability to overcome one of the most difficult obstacles that exists, the "what will people say?" syndrome. That being said, it's also important for me to emphasize their amazing courage and determination to go beyond the prognosis and earthly verdict passed on their marriage after suffering through one of the most difficult storms life can throw at you, choosing rather to believe God and His promises to overcome a crisis that many marriages today could not surpass. If you're looking for a book to help you heal the wounds of betrayal, rejection, and sin and show you the path toward freedom from anger, bitterness, and resentment, you've found it.

—René González
Author and singer
Senior Pastor, Iglesia Casa de Júbilo, PR

Since the day we met more than 25 years ago, I've admired Ricardo Rodríguez's voice. In fact, On many occasions I've jokingly mentioned that every time I hear him sing I feel the overwhelming urge to open up a Mexican taco stand and just quit singing. His voice is surely privileged, but what takes it even further is the anointing God has placed over his life. His songs have broken me before God in ways I can't describe. His latest production, *Huele a Lluvia* ("Smells Like Rain") has left me engulfed in loving and thankful tears before the Lord and blessed my life like no other project has in recent memory. Whenever I long to feel grateful and in love with God once more, I listen to it over and over again. Anointing goes hand in hand with brokenness. The state of complete dependence created by adversity causes God to pour His oil over our lives, and only in those moments of tribulation can we be filled by Him. After reading this book, I understood why Ricardo carries an anointing above many others. His testimony of brokenness and restoration is one that shook my life. What great examples of repentance and forgiveness we find in the Rodríguezes' marriage. I'm convinced that this book will bring freedom and restoration to thousands of marriages the enemy has tried to destroy. Through the experience lived by Susana and Ricardo, God will heal many.

Their honesty and transparency touched the very fibers of my being, for it requires great courage to be transparent. These two individuals are generals in God's army, for after having been in the trenches, they have learned from their mistakes and now stand firm to fight the enemy. I'm proud to be their friends and co-servants and honor them as great ones of our faith.

I pray that God speaks to you through Susana and Ricardo as you read their miraculous story of redemption that is their testimony.

—Marcos Witt,
Author and award-winning psalmist

WHAT IF WE
START OVER?

WHAT IF WE START OVER?

RICARDO AND SUSANA RODRÍGUEZ

RICARDO & SUSANA
RODRÍGUEZ

PARAEL
PRODUCCIONES

This publication is translated from Spanish under the title *¿Y Si Comenzamos de Nuevo?*, copyright © 2016 by Susana & Ricardo Rodríguez, ISBN: 978-1-62136-950-9, published by Casa Creación, a Charisma Media company. This English edition is published by permission.

Visit the author's website at www.ricardorodriguez.com

Editorial Development by LM Editorial Services | lydia@lmeditorial.com
Edited by Amanda Quain | quain.amanda@gmail.com
Cover Design by Melanie E Morales | melanie.e.morales@gmail.com
Cover Photos by Héctor Torres | Shoin Studios

International Standard Book Number: 978-1-5136-3810-2
E-book ISBN: 978-1-5136-3811-9

First print edition: August 2018

Printed in the United States of America

DEDICATION

WE DEDICATE THIS BOOK TO our princesses, Madison and Miabella, who have been not only a blessing to our lives but a daily reminder of God's overwhelming faithfulness and undeterred love. His plans, although sometimes delayed, always produce spectacular results that, without a doubt, surpass even the most impossible of dreams and greatest of expectations.

It is the profound desire of our hearts that as you read Mommy and Daddy's story you too can arrive at the conclusion that:

> Love is fought for and defended, embraced and released,
> It lives in the heart but with actions is seen,
> Forgives and forgets, and can once again grow,
> To a bright crimson flame with one ember of hope.

Above all, never ever forget that God always has a plan. He never fails!

We love you, Miabella and Madison!

Mommy and Daddy

ACKNOWLEDGEMENTS

FAMILY, in the divine sense of the word, is one of the most beautiful gifts God has ever granted us. It serves as a safe refuge in the midst of the storm, providing peace and assurance when the winds and waves of life rise up to batter our fragile souls. It is a hiding place of love and compassion, where hope and healing are freely given to help us overcome the worst failures of our lives. It's where strong embraces and kind words are found, words that motivate you never to give up but instead to fight through thick and thin for your dreams. Our family has lived up to and surpassed every aspect of this definition, and for that we are eternally grateful.

We would like to thank them all, beginning with our parents, Miguelina Rodríguez and Oralia and Horacio Tamayo, who have been examples of inspiring faith and overwhelming love during the most difficult moments of our lives.

Rachel and Hamlet Díaz, thank you for your friendship and courage, and for showing us there are battles worth fighting.

Mery Parenzuela, Llily and Sam Fitzpatrick, Mauricio and Viviana Tamayo, and Odenia Meléndez, thank you for the support and love displayed throughout the years.

A special thank you to Norma Rodríguez, Ricardo's sister, who day after day has shown us what it means to live a grateful life full of joy and happiness, regardless of the pitfalls and hardships life inevitably brings. Always with her beautiful smile and incomparable passion for her brother's music, she's an inspiration to all. We love you!

Thank you to our friends:

Luis and María Fernández, for believing in our ministry and motivating us to write our love story.

Isaac and Lyssie Hernández, for the many years of friendship and unconditional support.

Judy Rojas, for being the definition of a true friend.

Pastor Julio Landa, for the words of hope and comfort that calmed the turbulent waters of the soul.

Pastors Aner and Vivian Morejón, for the example shown of restoration and healing.

Luciano Rodríguez, whose perfectly timed gift of the book *Freedom of Forgiveness* (*Perdonar para ser libre*) by David Augsburger changed the script of our lives.

Pastor Omayra Font and her store Marki for the beautiful dresses our girls are wearing.

Héctor Torres (Shoin Photography Studios), for always giving the best of you, your talent and friendship.

Ruthie Rosario (makeup and hair), for always surpassing our expectations.

Lydia Castro Morales, for believing in us from the very start and guiding us through this journey with excellence and divine inspiration.

Amanda Quain, for smoothing out and polishing the rough edges of this effort of love, and in doing so, helping us impact a whole new world.

Pastors Frank and Zoyla López (JWC), sent by God and arriving right on time into to our hearts to confirm this new season in our lives and to show us how much our story needed to be heard. Thank you! Thank you! Thank you!

Above all, we thank You, Lord, for turning the vile and despised into something precious and useful and for giving us the opportunity to be examples of your love and compassion.

*We come to love not by finding a perfect person
but by learning to see an imperfect person
perfectly.*

—SAM KEEN

(1931–) Author, professor, and American philosopher

CONTENTS

FOREWORD

IT IS IMPERATIVE as leaders to remind ourselves constantly that we represent a God of love, restoration, and mercy. As a pastor, Susana and Ricardo's story has confronted me. Every chapter has been an impressive lesson on how to pastor with love and how to react correctly when someone makes mistakes. As clergy we invest time, energy, and prayer in keeping our flock within God's path and purpose, but sometimes our expectations are misplaced and our hopes are misguided. We are wrong if we assume that as Christians we're exempt from making egregious offenses and terrible mistakes. The grave error that Susana committed was, without a doubt, a sin, and as leaders, we expect it not to occur in church. But in reality we are all very capable of sinning and quite adept at doing terrible things.

A marriage in which the husband and wife love and serve God is top priority for the enemy to deceive, confuse, and destroy. Satan is an expert in deception, and we are all vulnerable to his false opportunities. If you look at how it all fell apart in Ricardo and Susana's marriage, you'll see it was not Susana's transgression that created the rift. Ricardo's absence at home—caused by the lack of balance between marriage and ministry, the responsibilities and demands of the church, and the inability to properly prioritize—created a void in their relationship and a wedge through which Satan was able to attack. We cannot forget that we are in a constant spiritual battle, that we have an enemy who has come to steal, kill, and destroy.

Thankfully, however, our God is one of grace and true opportunities. The power of Christ is perfected in our weaknesses, and that which Satan has conspired to destroy, God can turn into a fountain of inspiration and a message to save millions. His grace cancels the fruits of deceit and confusion, and in it we again find the correct path and true north. The more we experience the restoration and grace of our God, the more His love, paternity, and the power of the cross is revealed. There is nothing He cannot restore. It's a mystery. I've seen how God, in order to fix a disastrous situation, will sometimes allow you to get to zero, and from zero He then creates something beautiful.

Ricardo and Susana have one of those real-life stories where God's grace was greater than human error, pride, and statistics. But that same grace is also for us pastors and leaders to give without exception. As pastors, more than anyone, we are required to care for the fold with love, mercy, and the wisdom of the Holy Spirit, always expressing the character of our God—one of infinite grace from the Father of new beginnings. Let us care for the flock in the same way Jesus did.

In reading this book, my perception of how to react before the sins and mistakes of my own congregation changed completely. I recall that during same week in which I was reading the chapter in which Susana talks about how she was cast aside by everyone who found out about her sin, a member of my church confessed to me their own infidelity and how their spouse had uncovered it. As a pastor I had invested time, prayer, and care into this couple, and when I found out that I too had been lied to, along with the spouse, my reaction was one of anger, judgment, and renouncement to continue my commitment to the restoration of their marriage. However, God confronted me and placed in my heart the conviction to engage them with mercy, taking into account the repentance and forgiveness in their hearts. I'm grateful that Ricardo's and Susana's open testimony was able to convict me and remind me that as pastors, it is very important for us to provide everyone spiritual guidance and pastoral care without prejudgment. That care can help close wounds in hearts and provide the restoration necessary for them to one day be completely healed.

If you're a pastor, mentor, father, mother, or spiritual leader, this book will inspire you to grow in God's grace and mercy and be instruments useful in God's hands. He needs us to care, heal, and restore. Let us never discard, judge, nor turn our backs on a brother who falls, but in turn have the maturity to acknowledge that we are all vulnerable and never to forget that one day it might be us. As leaders, let us always be willing to offer mercy and hope and to be a living expression of God's grace. Even when the person doesn't deserve it, let us be examples of God's unconditional love.

Keep in mind that by the way you respond to someone else's sin you can either spark the process of restoration in their lives or create further pain and worsen the wound. Our words and attitudes are decisive. The worst mistake is to judge. The greatest virtue is to manifest mercy and inspire the person to have a change of heart and a willingness to turn from sin. God is capable of healing any and all situations. He doesn't discard, and there's nothing impossible for Him.

Let us learn from Ricardo's and Susana's example. Today they serve together and share their testimony in front of multitudes. From the worst thing that could've happened in their lives, God restored them and placed an anointing over them to remind us that He never discounts anyone one and that He didn't die to judge the world but instead to save it and restore the fallen and broken. There is no sin God will not forgive, and there is nothing impossible for Him. He is the God that restores, and seeing the restoring power in action is to experience the same expression of love from the Father.

I believe with all my heart that this book is prophetic; an instrument of healing that will be used by the Holy Spirit for generations to come. The sincerity and transparency with which the authors have poured themselves out throughout these pages has made it a unique and excellent read. We believe in this project and recommend it with all our hearts.

Susana and Ricardo, I congratulate you! Thank you for the courage it took to write it and for giving us this precious jewel. Your testimony will save multitudes of marriages and will bring a greater revelation of the power of God's grace and mercy. Thank you for being pioneers in bringing this topic to the forefront, as the message about the importance of prioritizing our families and caring for our marriages has long been missing, especially in the Latin-American church. You are examples that we gain nothing from saving the world and losing our marriages.

Above all, thank you for opening your lives to the world in an effort to reach it with the restoring power of our heavenly Father. Jesus spoke of this when He said, "Love your neighbor as yourself" (Matt. 22:39, NIV).

—FRANK LÓPEZ
Author of *Bienaventurados los discípulos* [Blessed Are the Disciples]
Senior Pastor of Jesus Worship Center, Doral, FL

INTRODUCTION

THERE ARE SOME STORIES that are told with a nostalgia and pride and others that are shared with paralyzing fear and cautious trepidation. I can safely say that ours encompasses all these and more.

Our story is one of love, faith, and perseverance. It is at the same time as common as any other and as unique as you'll ever find. It is a garden that was wilted and decaying from sin but was brought back to life by the supernatural dew of God's amazing grace.

The Bible says that the wages of sin is death, that everything you sow you shall reap. Whenever I heard those words as a child I always transported myself to a future time and place, that moment when we will all stand before our Creator and, with our iniquities exposed, have judgment passed upon us. If you accepted Jesus as your personal Savior, you will inherit eternal life; but if you pass on that decision, you will be held accountable, paying for your mistakes and transgressions with endless suffering and permanent separation from God. This was something terrible and distant, so I thought. But sin also has immediate repercussions, charging mercilessly for our all that which, in secret, we assumed would be free. Unfortunately, sooner or later, the bill always arrives.

It's hard now to remember the details of the moment I found out my relationship with Susi would be forever changed, seeing as it was something I fought so hard to forget. But I can honestly say the day began like any other. There weren't any grey clouds, nor was it raining, like you see in the movies. No melancholy soundtrack played in the background while my wife made her way to the office where I blissfully waited, unaware and unprepared for the storm that laid ahead. Everything seemed normal. Never in my wildest dreams did I imagine the debt was overdue and the amount would be so high. I learned that day that mistakes are not always exclusively paid by the guilty; sometimes the innocent and unsuspecting victims wind up getting stuck with the check.

"I've been unfaithful."

Those were the words that I heard from my wife—words that, in an instant and with immediate and agonizing results, buried our marriage, scorched our dreams, and put an end to the hope of a happy life together. We were now just another statistic, another failed couple.

It's incredible how just three words can painfully pierce a heart, killing every dream and happiness in the blink of an eye. I can't adequately describe the emotions that came over me when I understood my reality would never be the same and that my once-fairytale life was now a cruel nightmare from which there was no waking up.

With that short phrase I learned firsthand how the consequences of sin bring condemnation, anguish, and death, both in the spiritual realm as well as the physical one. As much as you might ask for forgiveness, the damage shatters the soul, leaving profound wounds that take time—and effort—to heal.

Opening up our hearts and revealing the intimate details of our lives is no easy task, so consequently, we do it with caution, finding strength and refuge in God's grace, forgiveness, and mercy. That aside, we are motivated by the possibility that maybe someone, somewhere, somehow might read our story and embrace the essence of these words: "There is nothing impossible for God!" (Luke 1:37, author's paraphrase).

It is our hearts' desire that all people come to know that regardless of their circumstances, what others have said, how deep the abyss they have found themselves in, or their own self-doubt, they too can come to know the God who can heal the wounds and restore the broken hearts caused by the sins and pains of infidelity, abandonment, and rejection within a marriage. If by reading it just one person is moved to embrace the possibility that He can do a miracle in their lives and, by doing so, help them to attain the unattainable—reconciliation—to share it is our privilege and divine responsibility.

By no means are we experts in marriage counseling, nor perfect enough to suggest anyone follow our footsteps. In fact, our mistakes and imperfections are without a doubt markers to be avoided at all costs. Yet, we humbly offer you through our straightforward and transparent recollection the unique perspective that only those who have crossed the arid desert of a broken marriage can have. Having crossed that desert, we want to make it abundantly clear that, first, you are not alone; second, you can make it to the other side with a stronger, healthier, and completely healed marriage; and third, while we understand what you're going through, it is far more important that you know God understands—and He has a plan!

Rest assured, His blueprint is perfect for you, not just so you can make it out of the deserts of your life but that you might come out on the other side victorious and grateful, with a greater and more profound understanding of His unwavering love and life-changing power. He not only can but wants to and is patiently waiting for an opportunity to glorify Himself in the failures of your life.

There is life on the other side of the desert of broken dreams and shattered hearts. That's because when repentance meets forgiveness, everything is possible.

But I'm getting ahead of myself. Let's start from the beginning. This is our love story.

—RICARDO RODRÍGUEZ

Chapter 1

A LOVE STORY REVEALED

By Susana and Ricardo

(**Susana**): "Hello, my name is Susana Mabel." Those were the words my father heard in a dream when I was still in my mother's womb. It's mind blowing to imagine that God was involved in my life way before I was even born. That not only did He know me by name but also every proud accomplishment—and shameful misstep—I would ever take on this earth.

I was born on a Sunday, literally in church. My father, being a pastor in Líbano, Tolima, Colombia, took ministry and its responsibilities very seriously. He never missed a day, and neither would my mom, even when she was in active labor with me. The night I was born, like every other night, my father arrived early to church. It wasn't a long trip, seeing as they lived in a room attached to the church itself. It was there in that room where my mom, grudgingly and afraid, stayed resting since the contractions were beginning and she felt I would arrive at any moment. The midwife got there just in time, and no sooner had the service started than the announcement was made as if from a Sunday school bulletin: "Susana Mabel Tamayo has arrived!"

In 1973, when I was at the age of three, my parents, looking to give us a better opportunity and the life they never had, packed up their humble belongings, left friends and family behind, and with only fifty dollars in their pockets and their hearts full of hopes and dreams, boarded a plane to the USA. We landed in Miami, Florida, and there began our new life.

1

Living in a foreign country is in no way an easy task. The immigrant's struggle to survive is constant and in many ways underappreciated and misunderstood. You have to live it to understand it. There are moments of hunger—both physical and emotional—rejection, and self-doubt, and as if that were not enough, there is always the nostalgia waiting for you at the end of a long, hard day of grueling work, like a long-lost love calling out from a distant and unreachable land. Even so, we found strength and comfort in our faith, understanding that God's provision was never far away. I began to grow up in a loving home where God was first and hope always followed.

The End of Innocence

For years we lived in a low-income neighborhood, a place looked upon by most with fear and contempt. Even so, for me it was a little piece of heaven. I thoroughly enjoyed my childhood, never truly realizing how poor we were or fully understanding the dangers that awaited me just outside my door. I remember clearly how much I loved talking to God in my free time. There was an open field next to my house, and I would lie there on the grass for hours looking up at the clouds and asking Him questions. Sometimes I would make up songs and sing to Him. I would pass the time soaking in His presence, and it filled me with joy.

Nevertheless, danger and tragedy where never far away. Living where we lived always kept us exposed to crime and happenings that would quickly rob us of our innocence. I remember one muggy summer day, the kind that only those who live in Florida can relate to. Some of us kids in the neighborhood decided to go swimming in a canal next to the projects. There weren't any public pools available where we lived, so the canals around our homes became the neighborhood hangout and what we always used to cool off. Unfortunately, the canals were also used as garbage dumps and were always full of old furniture, broken appliances, and even cars that the owners had no more use for. One of the kids who was swimming in the canal that day was a friend and schoolmate of mine. I remember him diving into the deep end of the canal as we all cheered him on, but to our shock and dismay, he never came back up.

Everyone began to scream and dive in to look for him, including my father, who happened to be driving by, but to no avail. They couldn't find him. When the authorities arrived, they quickly put on their scuba gear and finally found him stuck in an old refrigerator at the bottom of the canal. I'll never forget the look of anguish and despair on my father's face when he realized what had just happened. It was a tragedy that transformed us all, and looking back I can honestly say that was the beginning of the end of my childhood.

This tragedy left me with a profound sadness and great insecurity. Soon after, I recall asking my father, "Dad, what happens when someone dies?" He explained to me that we all have a soul, and before we die we must make a very important decision: whether or not to accept Jesus as our personal Savior. This decision would be the difference between going to heaven or hell. He explained to me all about heaven and the sacrifice that Jesus made on the cross to allow us entry into God's kingdom, as well as about hell and how horrible and void of peace and happiness it was. Being only eight years old, it was all very confusing to me, so I got on my bike and rode to my favorite place. There on the grass I laid down and cried inconsolably. Once again speaking to God, I opened up my heart, and in that moment I accepted Jesus as my personal Savior. I understood that I couldn't live without Him, that wherever this life would take me, He had to be at the center of it. I had always loved talking to God, and now I had the confidence that His Spirit would be with me always, wherever I might go.

A HEALING MIRACLE

From a very young age I suffered with asthma and dealt with debilitating attacks that would press against my chest till I was literally out of breath. In those moments my parents would quickly rush me to the doctor, where I would be administered a shot of cortisone to help me breathe again. This process, after having repeated itself many times, created an issue with my weight that soon began to affect my self-esteem in a negative way. I developed a complex that slowly made the smile and joy that represented so much of who I was fade away. I became an introvert, hiding within myself while avoiding the mirror as much as possible.

My parents, with all their love and good will, never quite understood what it was I truly needed—a hug, an "I love you," maybe even a "You are a beautiful princess." These were words that I so desired but that I seldom, if ever, heard. Sometimes what did get mentioned worsened my situation. My father had an obsession with oral hygiene. He always had us brush before and after every meal and obviously when we woke up and went to sleep. One of his favorite phrases was, "The only beautiful thing you have is your teeth. Take care of them!" In hindsight I understand what his intentions were. He had suffered a lot with his own teeth and wanted us not to have the same problems he did, but in the moment those words pressed on my heart and weighed down my already low self-esteem. I grew up feeling ugly and for a long time thinking that the only good thing I had was my smile.

There are many studies that reveal the profound influence a father has on his daughter's self-worth. Some statistics conclude that up to the age of twelve, 90 percent of a girl's self-esteem is given by her father. Fathers who shine a light on the talents, interests, and accomplishments of their daughters produce young women who are emotionally healthy and sure of themselves, while those who focus their attention on only the physical attributes create insecurity, a feeling of unworthiness, and a constant need to be reassured later on in life. Young girls who grow up without a father tend to have problems with self-esteem, contrary to those who have an active father figure in their upbringing. They, in turn, grow up confident and sure of themselves.[1]

It is of the utmost importance as fathers to let your daughters know that they are loved and to encourage them in their endeavors with words of affirmation that not only are they beautiful on the outside but, more importantly, on the inside, where it truly matters. This prepares them to be successful under God's perfect plan as they walk into a world that will, most likely, judge them for their appearance and not their character. They will know who they are: daughters of a loving and wonderful God, always precious in His eyes. Many times we encounter children whose parents are so busy providing for the material needs that they tragically overlook the emotional and spiritual emptiness that can only be filled with attention, love, and encouragement.

Arriving home one night after our local church service, I began to feel ill. I recognized the symptoms. I could feel my lungs tightening up, and with every passing second I was finding it harder and harder to breathe. It was another asthma attack, but this one was more severe than any other I'd had before. In my despair I called out to my parents, who came quickly and began to pray over me.

Asthma is such a terrible illness. If it's bad for an adult, it's horrible for a child. The fear and despair caused by not being able to fill your lungs with air creates an overwhelming anxiety, which in turn makes everything that much worse. It's a vicious and deadly cycle.

That night nothing seemed to be working for me, and my parents, sensing the dire situation, decided to rush me to the nearest emergency room. On our way there I honestly thought I wasn't going to make it. Every breath was forced, and it felt as though my body struggled to live.

My parents couldn't disguise their frantic and worried faces. Somehow, though, this trip to the hospital seemed longer than others, and soon I realized that we'd left the hospital miles behind. Following this unknown course—and leaving behind whatever medical hope existed of me getting better—they continued driving with urgency. There were other plans that night. My father was going to put his faith in action and once and for all entrust his daughter to the hands of the greatest Doctor of all. He heard about an old-fashioned camp meeting in an adjacent city where God was using a pastor to heal many people who had been ill. He arrived with great expectations.

My father carried me in his arms through the doors of that old church. Desperate and fearful, we both managed to get to the front, where everyone was awaiting prayer and their miracle. As the preacher laid his hands on my forehead, I felt a rush of heat all over my body and my once-closed lungs open up. That first breath was like a fish back in water. I couldn't believe it. God had healed me! Our faith was energized, and our hearts were eternally thankful. From that moment on, I never again had another severe asthma attack. I was no longer the delicate little girl who couldn't run and jump and do all the other things her peers were doing. I had become a living example of the healing power of our God!

First Love

Like most other young girls growing up in the suburbs of a major city, I had my own personal struggles and challenges to deal with as the years went by, but during that time church remained an important part of my life. That, as well as my fear of God, kept me from making the same mistakes my peers were constantly making. Though I wasn't perfect, I always tried to honor my parents and God by staying on the narrow road. I can honestly say that their prayers and the teachings they provided strengthened my heart and prepared me for those difficult adolescent years. The Bible says in Proverbs 22:6, "Train up a child in the way he should go: and when he is old, he will not depart from it". I believe that is the reason why I'm here today to tell this story of restoration and victory.

I began to visit a church in Miami that would always invite local singers and bands for youth concerts. One day they invited a group called Newlife comprised of four musicians from a nearby church. They had their music playing on the local radio and were quickly becoming one of the most popular bands in town. The day of the concert I was accompanied by a young man whom I had met in church. Our friendship was beginning to blossom into something more serious. We arrived at the venue early to find a good seat and enjoy the concert, but to our surprise, Newlife was more popular than we anticipated, and the place was full. We managed to find seats in the back and waited for the concert to start. As the music began to play and the people stood up, I heard a voice coming from the speakers that stood out from the rest. It was a beautiful, strong, and clear voice that melodically filled the room with a message of God's love and mercy. The atmosphere was amazing, and the Spirit of God was moving and speaking to our hearts.

Halfway through the concert the weirdest thing happened. My friend, who I noticed had been strangely quiet, leaned into my ear and whispered the words, "I have a feeling you're going to marry the lead singer." I looked at him with a surprised and slightly bothered face and asked him, "Why would you say that?" He simply responded, "I feel it in my heart." It was something out of left field that caught me totally off guard. I didn't know the singer, nor could I see him well from where we were. It all seemed pretty absurd at the time, though later on I would come to find out it was more prophetic than absurd.

Time passed, and in 1991 a close friend of mine asked me to be one of the bridesmaids in her wedding. The wedding rehearsal was at her church, which soon after I began to visit regularly. I loved the young people at that church and quickly made friends there. One day the youth pastor invited me to a concert that was taking place the following weekend. Of course, I said yes. Music was, and continues to be, a very important part of my life, so concerts were always something I was up for. When I arrived at the church and walked through the doors I was pleasantly surprised to find out that Newlife was the invited band that night. At the end of the concert the piano player invited me to meet up with them at a local restaurant, and it was there that I formally met the lead singer, Ricardo Rodríguez, for the first time.

From the first hello I could feel there was a connection between us, a spark that made us both nervous and anxious. However, communication was cumbersome, and that made every passing moment incredibly awkward. We were both very shy, which was a hurdle that was becoming obviously difficult to overcome. He hardly said two words to me, and I could barely glance at him without quickly turning away. Nevertheless, in the midst of all that discomfort, I managed to find something to focus on: his hands. I found them very attractive, probably because in my shyness that's all I would look at. The guys in the band did their best Cupid impression and forced us to sit together with the intention of us getting to know each other better and maybe exchanging phone numbers. The plan didn't work, and the night finished with a simple "good-bye" and "It was nice to meet you."

I thought that was the end of it, but a few weeks later I once again received an invitation from the youth pastor to attend one of their events. This time it was a football game the church was organizing. What I didn't know is that Ricardo was the captain and quarterback of the team, so when I arrived at the park, I was presently surprised to find him there. At the end of the game Ricardo came up to me and asked if I would like to have dinner with him that night, and doing my best to hide my excitement, I quietly said yes.

The dinner lasted for several hours, during which we spoke about music, God, family, and many other seemingly important subjects. When the night came to a close, he nervously asked me for my number, and I happily obliged. We said our good-byes and went our separate ways.

My hopes became reality when he called me the next day. I'd been anxious to hear his voice again, so when I answered and he said, "Hello," I couldn't contain myself. I don't know if he noticed my joy upon hearing his voice, but it didn't seem to matter anyway. We listened to each other, understood each other, and shared so much that first night that we wound up hanging up at 5:00 am. Even from the beginning there was something different about us, something more profound and spiritual that joined us at a deeper level. That first conversation sealed our friendship, and from that very moment I knew that what we had shared that night hadn't been a superficial, run-of-the mill phone call but something unique and worth building upon.

As our friendship continued I found myself looking more and more forward to whatever time we could spend together in person or on the phone. My job was very demanding. I worked in a photographic laboratory at the ophthalmology department at the Bascom Palmer Eye Institute. There I would spend most of the day in a dark room with chemicals, processing hundreds of film rolls so that the doctors could determine what was wrong with their patients. Those days seemed endless and the hours slow to pass as I anxiously waited for the clock to reach four o'clock so that I could rush home and talk to Ricardo once again. (There were no cell phones in those days, so commutation required much more patience and effort on our parts). Our relationship was quickly growing into something special, and just a few months after that first phone call, with the permission of my parents, we officially and exclusively started dating.

A SPECIAL NIGHT

I was twenty-one, and he was twenty-four, and we were getting along great. I loved to go see him sing in local events and marveled at the talent God had bestowed upon him, not just as a singer but also as an amazing songwriter. Six months after having met, he prepared a magical night for us at a fancy restaurant in Bayside Miami. We ate and afterward took a stroll throughout the marina in hopes of taking a boat ride under the stars. We found gondolas, like the ones they have in Venice, Italy, but as we approached to ask about the possibility of taking a romantic ride in one of them, the owner put up the closed sign. Ricardo was disappointed but continued searching for something to ride.

All the boats were closed, so we walked toward the city, where he noticed some horse-drawn carriages had been trotting around. When we approached the gentleman attending the horses, I began to feel ill, and no sooner had we sat on top of the carriage than we had get back down on account of how bad I felt. Ricardo had tried so hard to make the night romantic, but it was to no avail.

I felt my body getting hot and knew I was suffering from a high fever, but I couldn't find the moment to tell him, so we just kept searching. We wound up at Hallandale Beach, close to his parents' house.

Ricardo asked if we could walk a bit down the beach, and so we did. I still hadn't mentioned to him how bad I was feeling, so I tried to keep up and make the best of it. After a while we found a lifeguard station and stopped for a quick rest. I clearly remember the next moment like it was yesterday. Ricardo got down on one knee and declared his love for me. He told me he was sure that I was the one for him and that life without me was impossible. There, under moonlit skies, with the ocean breeze around us, and the soundtrack of waves crashing in the distance, he asked me to be his wife. I was surprised if not shocked to hear those words—it was the last thing I imagined!—but with tears in my eyes and a heart full of hope, I said yes.

What I felt that night was overwhelming and without a doubt one of the most memorable and emotional moments I had ever experienced. I was going to be the wife of Ricardo Rodríguez, a man who loved me and his family with all his heart but, more importantly, loved God.

In the weeks that followed we began to plan the wedding quickly and to look for a place to live and call our own. The first thing I bought was my wedding gown—a beautiful white dress lined with pearls and all the satin and lace any little girl could ever dream of. Every day I would stare at it and dream of how my life would be alongside Ricardo, how many children we would have, and what they would look like. Everything was set for a joyous and wonder-filled future together.

TRAGEDY STRIKES

(**Ricardo**): One day after getting home from work, my father was quickly sent to the neighborhood pharmacy to get medicine for the cold that I had recently been diagnosed with. I was barely two months old, and my parents weren't taking any chances with my health. They had gone through a very difficult time with my sister, Norma, since her birth. She arrived purple with little to no signs of breathing, and unfortunately neither the doctors nor the nurses attending her were able to assess the situation on time and properly treat it to prevent any long-term effects. She suffered severe brain damage and was given a bleak prognosis. Her early years were full of doctor visits and many sleepless nights for my parents. At the age of two my mom was told to prepare for the inevitable fact that my sister wouldn't make it past her twelfth birthday. (She is currently fifty-four years old at the writing of this book.)

Me, on the other hand, I was born weighing almost eleven pounds. As per my mother, I was an impressive sight to behold, so big and fat. She tells me that the nurses who had failed to treat my sister on time felt responsible and indebted to her; therefore, they took every precaution to make sure I would be born without any complications. They gave her vitamins and everything else imaginable to assure a healthy baby. As you can imagine, I was well taken care of from the very beginning.

The day I came down with a cold, my father, like any other compassionate and loving father, didn't think twice before getting back on his motorcycle after a long, hard day of work and heading out to the local pharmacy to get me my medicine. At the corner down our street as my father patiently waited for the light to turn green, a truck lost control and violently hit him while he sat on his motorbike. He perished that day laying on the pavement just a few blocks away from his house. They tell me his last words were, "Oh, my God."

He was twenty-seven years young the day he died, leaving my mom widowed at the age of twenty-nine with two young children—one at the tender age of just fifty-four days old, the other needing round-the-clock medical attention for the rest of her recently prognosticated short life.

My father didn't have a chance to say good-bye to his family. There weren't any inspiring words given before his last breath, nor a final, loving embrace to his wife and children as he closed his eyes for the last time. He passed away alone, just a few yards away from where everyone who ever mattered to him sat patiently waiting. There wasn't time to reconcile differences. There was no opportunity to ask forgiveness from those who he had failed or offended nor forgive those who had done the same. Time had expired, and whatever accounts weren't settled in that moment would remain that way forever.

That accident, without a doubt, left my family grasping for answers from a God they always considered to be loving and benevolent. But the answers never arrived. There wasn't any reasoning with the finality of death, no way to humanly comprehend nor justify such a horrible and painful tragedy. Those who surrounded my mother wanted to console her by giving her some kind of emotional help, but regardless of how hard they tried, she remained inconsolable. It was only after she received a letter from a distant friend that she began to find her way out of the terrible abyss of despair and pain that had become her life. The letter simply read, "There is no pain on earth that heaven cannot heal." Those words filled her with hope and encouraged her to grasp hold of her faith like never before. She understood that God had not forsaken her, and ultimately, He had a plan.

LIFE LESSONS THAT ENDURE

My mother never remarried. She remained a widow and focused her life on raising her children with God's help and the help of my grandmother, her mother-in-law. My grandma never left her alone. Even as my mother left Cuba, my grandma accompanied her, forsaking everything and everyone to make sure her daughter-in-law had the help she needed to raise her children.

We left Cuba when I was five years old and my sister, Norma, was nine, arriving in Madrid, Spain, in 1972. No sooner had we gotten settled than my mom and grandma began to work closely with a local church. They were both a valuable part of the evangelical movement in Spain in those early years, a time in which Protestant Christians were still being persecuted under then-dictatorship of Francisco Franco.

As far back as I can recall, my life has been one of God and church, faith and trust, and prayer and provision. I come from the generation that would go to church from Monday through Saturday and twice on Sunday. It was the same generation that lived in the streets playing with friends, but when church time came, playtime was over. There weren't many valid excuses to miss church. If you were sick, it had to be a hospital-level sickness to stay home, and even then, if you got prayed for, it was church for sure.

After two years of living in Spain we traveled to California and settled in South Gate, a suburb close to Los Angeles. We lived there for four years. I learned to love tacos, enchiladas, huevos rancheros… I could go on and on. The cultural influences were molding my likes and dislikes, not just in food but in just about everything, especially in music. I began taking accordion lessons at the age of ten, and for a whole year I gave it all I had. In the end, though, I ultimately surrendered and fell in love with the instrument that would serve me as friend and companion for the rest of my life: the piano.

At the age of eleven we moved to Miami, Florida, the magic city. I'll never forget the moment I first laid eyes on those beautiful sandy beaches dotted by majestic palm trees swaying in the ocean breeze—nor the painful sunburn left behind by the scorching sun on my way-too-pale skin. Every day was a postcard day, and from the very beginning I felt it: there was no place I would rather live.

For the sake of transparency and perspective, I must make it clear that we actually lived in the neighborhood of Carol City, and even though the sun shined brightly during the day, at night it was a different story. My mother's purse was repeatedly stolen, and when it wasn't her purse, it was her car, or the house getting broken into. Every week something or someone different was assaulted or their property broken into. Nothing could be left outside without a lock and chain of some kind, a lesson I quickly learned when my brand-new bike, the one I had just received for Christmas, was stolen in front of our house as I ran in to get something to drink. All in all, looking back, I thank God for every one of those experiences, for through it all His protection and provision never waned.

High school was also a challenge. Although I was a good student, I always felt out of place and never truly bought into the whole high school experience. I gravitated more to all things church and music and found joy in immersing myself in gospel albums like Andraé Crouch and the Disciples, the Winans, the Imperials, and so many others that to this day greatly influence my singing and writing. Getting into trouble around the neighborhood also was never part of the plan. Living with two hard-working, strong women of God kept me from doing anything that would ever disappoint them.

MUSICAL BEGINNING

A few months after arriving in Carol City, my aunt Mery opened a small mission close to home. One day after hearing me play an old electric piano my mom had recently bought me, she decided I was going to be the official piano player at the newly opened church. I loved my aunt dearly, and her influence in my life has been immense, but in that moment I really thought she had lost it. I didn't know how to play half a song, let alone church hymns and/ or whatever else was required of a church pianist. I'd only taken a couple of piano lessons and wasn't prepared for the responsibility. But she, being a woman of faith and vision, insisted till I could no longer say no, and soon after I found myself learning those hymns as fast as I could.

I recall those first Sundays struggling to find what key the worship leader was singing in and failing miserably. I would've had a better chance at finding Noah's ark. It was a disaster of biblical proportions. At least it felt that way to me. I was embarrassed not only for me but also for everyone forced to witness and sadly hear the uncomfortable musical drama playing out every Sunday morning.

Having said that, something strange began to happen in the midst of all that stress. The responsibility that had been placed on my unwilling and unqualified shoulders started having a positive effect on me. Laziness and apathy were replaced by discipline and passion, characteristics required to be good at anything in life, especially a piano player/musical director, which I now was. Now, instead of spending a good portion of my days in the streets playing with my friends, I started separating more and more time for piano rehearsal. Music began to take a more important role in my life, and with time, the results were becoming more and more evident. Where once I couldn't find the key to a hymn, now I could play any hymn in any key with ease. My ears and my hands were in sync and agile enough to follow any worship leader, wherever his tone-deaf ears might lead. My aunt's challenge had been met, and her faith in me was rewarded with years of service in that humble church.

My family was never one of many means. Quite the contrary. They came from a humble and working-class background. My mother cleaned hotels in Spain, and upon arriving in the United States she, along with my grandmother, worked in clothing factories for as long as I can remember. We didn't have much but were never left wanting. God always provided. In fact, I truly never felt poor. For me, poverty, more than a financial state, was a state of mind, and in my mind I just didn't have money. I understood the place I lived, the clothes I wore, and the car I drove would not define me.

Therefore, although all of the places I lived in as a child and adolescent were low-income housing in poor neighborhoods, I never felt less than anyone. My mother and grandmother worked extremely hard to give me everything I needed and many times even what I wanted, and that effort—and the love that came with it—did not go unnoticed. It motivated me to stay on the righteous and narrow path. Many of my school and barrio friends from those years are now either dead, in jail, or living out their lives reminiscing about what could have been. In the end, it's not where you come from but how you finish that will define you.

Although I never had a father growing up, I had pastors and friends who guided me in my most vulnerable years. Even before I became involved in music ministry, my fondest memories and most cherished moments all happened in church. It was there I found refuge and allowed myself to hope and dream while surrounding myself with positive influences. One of those such influences was Pastor Melquíades Urgelles, who, along with his family, had an incredible influence in my transitional years from adolescence to a young man. Pastor Melquíades; his wife, Isabel; and their four children, Pablo, Isabelita, Melquis, and Wilmer, were all part of that hedge of protection that God, in His wisdom, formed around me. They were the brothers I never had but always dreamed of, and I will forever be grateful for their friendship and the love they offered me throughout those influential years.

ADVENTURES WITH NEWLIFE

I was barely eighteen years old when Pastor Melquíades's sons and I decided to form a musical group. In that group I would find the gang I never had, a place I could feel appreciated and just be myself. We dreamed of ministering and traveling throughout the world, but first we needed a name. After many failed attempts we settled on Newlife. The guys and myself, plus their cousins Gilberto and Domingo Gomero, were inseparable during those early years, during which we recorded three albums and fulfilled our dream of traveling abroad and all throughout the US.

I recall the bus we bought and customized to make it our official tour bus. It was a 1958 GMC heap of metal and rust that would leave us stranded more often than not. But it was ours, and we loved it. I could probably write another book just on the tours in that bus and the experiences surrounding all of it. I'll just say that we spent more time fixing it than driving it. We suffered through hunger and cold, rejections and embarrassments, but in hindsight I wouldn't change a thing. God was always present, and those experiences helped mold me into the minister I am today. At gas stations in east Los Angeles, bullrings in cities we couldn't pronounce, let alone spell, and big and small churches all over the United States, the passion was the same and the message never wavered. It was all about Jesus.

LOVE IS IN THE AIR

It was with Newlife that I had one of the most important encounters of my life. We were playing an event in Miami when, in the middle of the concert, I noticed a young girl dressed in white walk through the doors in the back of the church. I know what you're thinking: "Why were you looking at girls while you were worshiping?" My weak and non-spiritual response is simply this: God put her where my eyes were staring.

Her face was radiant, her beautiful brown eyes sparkling, and her long, curly hair made her stand out above all the rest. I needed to know who this girl was. But how could I approach this amazing young woman, being as shy as I was? Thank God for those wingmen who are always willing to lend a hand in those fleeting, once-in-a-lifetime moments. Gilberto, the other pianist in the group, knew this girl and noticed me staring at her, so he decided he would do his part to get us together by inviting us all to dinner at a fancy restaurant after the concert. It was an already genius idea made even better when he managed to have her and me sit together at the booth. It turns out the restaurant was really a Denny's, and there was nothing fancy about it. Furthermore, even with all his efforts, I don't think I said two words to her that night, and in the end I left there feeling as if the moment had been lost.

Thank God that a few weeks later I got a chance to redeem myself, and after one of our monthly football games with the youth of the church I invited her to dinner. It was there at the corner table in the Friday's by her house that I finally got to know Susi. Hearing her voice for only a few minutes during our conversation made me realize what a deep connection we had. Dinner was full of questions and declarations, jokes and opinions, and as the time passed away, so did my inhibitions and fears. As we said our good-byes we exchanged numbers and the promise to keep in touch. Soon after, when I did call her we talked until 5:00 am, and I knew from that moment on she was the one for me.

Chapter 2

SPEAK TO ME

by Susana Rodríguez

O UR BEGINNINGS AS man and wife were humble in every way. We had dreams and illusions, just like every other young couple, and a love that sustained us even through the scarcest of times. We, of course, aspired to have our own house, one we could fill with wonderful memories and maybe even one day raise our children in, but that particular dream seamed so far away for two kids who could barely make a car payment.

At first we moved into Ricardo's mom's house. She graciously allowed us to stay with her, along with his grandmother and sister, a few miles north of Miami. Still, every weekend without fail we would drive down to our church and visit my parents, who at the time were in the process of rebuilding their house after the devastation caused by hurricane Andrew. I recall on one of those weekends as Ricardo and I stood outside my parents' house listening to the hammering and sawing going on throughout what seemed to the be the whole neighborhood, a man on a tractor passed by and waved hello. That friendly gesture surprised us since it was given during a stressful and tumultuous time in Miami. There was so much construction in the neighborhood, so much insurance money flowing through, that everyone was on the defensive looking out for con artists and outright thieves. It made his wave that much more surprising and refreshing.

It also prompted us to begin to look deeper into the possibility of buying in that neighborhood. Ricardo and I had been looking for a house that had been damaged by the hurricane to purchase and fix up since they were going for very little money at the time. We had spoken to friends and neighbors asking for tips on damaged properties close by my mom's house, but it seemed we had waited too long and they were all but gone. So when this friendly man on a tractor passed by waving hello, we took it upon ourselves to ask one more time, this time of him, if he knew of any houses for sale nearby. To our surprise, he said, "Follow me."

After leading us just a couple of blocks down from my parents' house, he pointed to a totally destroyed house that was missing half the roof and most of the windows and doors. It was a sight to behold. We quickly jumped in through one of the windows and began to dream. It was a total disaster, abandoned and in disarray—but for us it was a gift from God. During that period in Miami many people couldn't get past the devastation Hurricane Andrew had left behind, and in their frustration and fear, they abandoned their homes without thinking twice. But one man's garbage is another man's treasure, and we had found our little piece of heaven.

A neighbor, seeing us inside the house, quickly approached and asked us what we were doing trespassing on private property. We responded by declaring in faith that we were interested in buying the house and would like to get in touch with the owner. She told us he had left the city but was selling the property, although she also mentioned we shouldn't get our hopes up since quite a few other parties had recently inquired about the house, and it probably had offers on it already. Nonetheless, we exchanged contact info.

That same day we called the number given to us and spoke to the lawyer handling the sale of the property. He let us know that the odds were indeed slim for us since others had already made offers on the house and there was no guarantee Ricardo and I could place our offer on time before a decision was made. But, he said, he'd keep us posted. We hung up feeling disillusioned yet assured that what God had for us no one could take away. In all honestly, being recently married and with zero savings and/or any readily available financial resources, the dream to own that house or any other was nothing more than an act of faith on a wing and a prayer. The Bible also says faith without works is dead, so we got to work.

The first thing we did was put Ricardo's car up for sale. It was a blue 1985 Jeep Renegade, which he totally adored. It was surprising to me to say the least that he was willing to sell it, but it showed me the dedication and passion with which he was going to attack this huge endeavor.

In the process of selling his Jeep I also learned something else about Ricardo. With all his talents and abilities, including his intellect and his ability to focus on the task on hand, he had his moments of airheadedness. This came to light one day when he left with my dad to park the Jeep at the busiest intersection near my parents' house, clearly intending to draw attention to it and therefore quickly sell it. He had cleaned it, leaving it like new, and had put a big For Sale sign on it. When he returned home, he seemed anxious and excited as he waited for the call with an offer for his prized possession. Oh, what a rude awakening he received when the phone rang and was told by a gentleman who had moments earlier stopped to look at the Jeep that he had left the keys in the ignition. Ricardo had left the car open with keys in the ignition and a For Sale sign on it. To make matters worse, this was in one of the busiest and most unsafe parts of South Miami. Needless to say, he hurried back to where he had parked the Jeep, praying it was still there and feeling incredibly embarrassed. Thank God no harm was done and all was as he had left it. When he finally returned home we laughed till our sides hurt and never again spoke of the whole dramatic episode. A few days later he managed to sell it for the exact amount we needed, and the first piece of the puzzle had fallen into place.

We began to pray for the miracle of the purchase of our home, asking our friends and family to join us in the pursuit of our dream. We knew it would be practically impossible for such a young couple with little to no means to be able to purchase a house so early on in their marriage, but Ricardo and I were trusting and believing that the house would be ours.

A few weeks later we received the long-awaited call from the owner. Ricardo spoke to him, and they decided to meet. The owner was a cordial man who, from the onset, asked us what our plans would be for the house. We let him know we had only been married three months and that it would be a dream for us to have a home of our own. We told him of our plans to work on the house ourselves, little by little fixing it up till we could move in and begin to make it a home. Ricardo let him know we'd been praying for a miracle and were confident God would have the last word. He looked at us with a smile on his face and said, "You're the couple I've been waiting to sell the house to." He was also a believer and felt directed not to sell the house to anyone except to the couple God led him to. The house was ours!

There aren't enough words to express the emotions we felt that day as we said our good-byes to the owner and walked back to our car. We looked at each other with tears in our eyes, and there, with admiration and gratefulness, we hugged and thanked our heavenly Father. That day marked a before-and-after moment in our lives. God had blessed us with security, and in the process He taught us a valuable lesson: dream big and never be afraid of the impossible!

We were left with only one car; a house without a roof, windows, or doors; and an incredible amount of work in front of us. But we were more than ecstatic and thankful for our little piece of heaven.

HUMBLE BEGINNINGS

With the purchase of our house, we moved in with my parents to be closer to the property and facilitate the rebuilding. During that time, Ricardo and I both worked at the Bascom Palmer Eye Institute, and I recall how every day we couldn't wait to get home to work on our house. Day and night, rain or shine—nothing could deter our desire to finish the work and finally move in. Every now and then friends would come over and help with the heavy lifting and the more complicated construction jobs, especially on the weekends, but Ricardo did most of it himself. He became an electrician, plumber, carpenter, tile installer, and everything else you could imagine necessary to turn a dream into reality.

It was a very busy and physically demanding time in both our lives, as I found myself right next to him, helping in any way I could every step of the way. I still remember Ricardo and I on the roof hammering shingles till the sun went down and the neighbors complained. Through it all it was very satisfying, as we knew that our house would soon be a home.

Only six months later, still with much work to do and with no furniture nor appliances, we moved into our home. At first we slept on a futon couch, which left our backs in knots and rendered us perpetually longing for a good night's sleep. Some time later we managed to procure a used stove and a refrigerator a friend of ours was throwing out. The kitchen sink was actually a mop sink for quite some time until we managed to get the kitchen fixed and a proper sink installed.

I wasn't very good at cooking at the time but always tried my best and would test different recipes on Ricardo in spite of our limited kitchen. One day I decided to make him a typical Puerto Rican plate called *pastelón*. I'd heard him mention to one of his friends that he really enjoyed it, so I would surprise him with a delicious meal. The only problem was, I was never really good at measuring ingredients; it was my Achilles heel. It was always a problem for me, and I would wind up cooking for an army most of the time. Long story short, we ate pastelón for a week at breakfast, lunch, and dinner. I don't think either one of us has tried it since.

Our house was as basic as you could get, and our lives were simple, but none of that mattered. We were together and as happy as could be.

A Business Opportunity

In 1994 our church offered me a job as assistant treasurer. I held that position for a few months until Ricardo and I decided to open a Christian bookstore in our neighborhood. We leased a space in a local strip mall and called our bookstore Lighthouse Bible Bookstore. The demands of preparing a bookstore for its grand opening were enormous, so Ricardo and I agreed to switch jobs. He would take my position in the church, and I would run the bookstore during the week. We acquired a loan—using our house as collateral—to invest in inventory and give the bookstore a running start.

There was so much to learn, and it was an immense undertaking just to get it ready for the grand opening, but when the day arrived the excitement was palpable. We always focused on being client centered, paying attention to detail, and timeliness in our orders from the beginning, and our strategy and efforts paid off. Business was slow at first, but soon word got out, and customers began to pour in. Our store was beginning to grow, and everything seemed perfect and under control.

Ricardo would leave me every day at the bookstore in the morning on his way to church. Soon he was not only doing accounting but also leading worship, which required him to participate in band and choir rehearsals at least three times a week. Around 7:00 pm he would return to help me close the store, and together we would return to church, grabbing a quick bite through a drive-through on our way back. Our world was getting complicated quickly, and time was becoming scarcer and more fleeting by the day. Still, we accepted that all in all this was our new life, and we were happy serving God in our new adventure.

In the bookstore I would spend my days attending the customers' needs and many times listening to their problems and personal struggles. This became a daily routine that quickly overwhelmed me. People began to see the bookstore as a place to unload their problems and receive counseling, something I wasn't ready for, nor had I signed up to deal with. It became a hospital for the needy and tired, and I found myself constantly attending to each and every one of those needs, even with the lack of experience I brought to the table.

There were so many stories and situations that impacted me during my time at the bookstore. There are different people and moments that I'll never forget, but one in particular stands out that truly left its mark. One ordinary morning as I was getting ready to open the store, I began to hear sirens at a distance. No sooner had I opened the door than a young man ran in with fear and despair in his eyes and knelt in front of me, wanting to confess to me his sins. He was sweating and seemed anxious, and it didn't take much for me to realize that he was the reason the sirens had been filling up the neighborhood. The police were searching for him.

He was desperate and alone, as was I, but an inexplicable calm fell over me, and I was overwhelmed with courage and compassion as I began to speak to his heart. I told him about God's forgiveness for those who repent and walk away from their sins, about His love and tender mercies, His underserving grace, and His profound compassion. I told him that it was all free, paid for by the blood of Jesus Christ. The young man began to cry inconsolably, and when he stood up he thanked me over and over again as he ran out of the store to confront the fate that awaited him. I never saw or heard from him again, but I'm sure that day he found, where he least expected it, peace in the midst of the storm and hope for his anxious soul. I have no doubt that God permitted our paths to cross, and it was He who spoke those words of encouragement and salvation through me. It never crossed my mind that sooner than I could imagine those same words would return to me to bring me back to life.

The bookstore continued to grow, and with time it had become my second home. There I would take refuge in the books and music that were always at my fingertips. I would meet people from different ethnicities, religions, races, and social strata on a daily basis.

I clearly recall a man in particular who had become a regular. Through a high school friend of mine I knew he was a high-ranking elder in the Jehovah's Witnesses, and seeing him come in always surprised me. He would arrive during lunchtime or late after work and always wore dark sunglasses. He would ask to see all the special edition Bibles and wound up ordering quite a few. I felt he was still looking for answers, not being satisfied with the ones he had been receiving. Speaking to him on various occasions, I discerned he had doubts and was confused about religion. I decided to simply pray for him and let the Word of God and the Holy Spirit do the rest. After all, how was I going to enter into theological discussions with an elder of the Jehovah's Witness church and someone who had read and studied religion way more than me? Yet, little by little I began to see a change in him. He became friendlier and more accessible over time as we continued to speak about the Bible. I knew that God was working in him. Little did he know that with every Bible he purchased, he was also taking home a prayer from a young girl who was interceding on his behalf. I felt it my mission and ministry to have him understand there was only one God, and only through Him would he ever find truth, knowledge, and salvation.

BUSY TIME

A few months after opening the bookstore, the church went through a huge growth spurt at the same time that Ricardo was tasked to lead worship in not just one service but all five on Sundays. This changed everything dramatically, as we practically lived in church. When we weren't at the bookstore, we were there, overwhelmed and overworked, tired and drained from all the responsibilities thrust upon us. As it often happens in positions of leadership, the problems began not from the workload but the lack of prioritizing.

We would barely see our family and friends in the little time we could spare, let alone have time for ourselves, and our relationship began to suffer. We longed to find a space in between for just us.

During this time in our marriage Ricardo and I decided to try and start a family. I was sure it would happen quickly. We had the names picked for a girl and a boy, and our illusions and dreams were in the clouds. However, months passed—and nothing. It was becoming more difficult than either of us expected. I became frustrated and disillusioned, and depression was slowly creeping in. All my friends had gotten pregnant and were already on their second or third child, and here I was designated the undesirable position of being the only one who couldn't have babies.

My days became intense and monotonous simultaneously, and my emotions told the same story. I began to feel sad and alone without Ricardo. His time was preoccupied with more important responsibilities I thought, and there was little left for me at the end of his long day at church and the bookstore. I stopped being the wife who wanted to cook for her husband and instead became the one who complained about fast food and drive-thrus. I stopped seeing my home as the gift from God it truly was and more like an empty house, boring and mundane. I no longer weighed what I had with a grateful heart but instead placed it alongside others' to make a comparison, and it always left me wanting more. A grateful heart is the key to living a happy and fulfilled life, and being able to see God's favor and blessing in my life had always been a part of my DNA since I was a little girl. But something was happening inside me, and my world was slowly turning grey and losing its value. Nothing I or Ricardo did brought me joy anymore.

Giving thanks always for all things unto God and the Father in the name of our Lord Jesus Christ.

—EPHESIANS 5:20

*Not that I speak in respect of want: for I have
learned, in whatsoever state I am, therewith to be
content. I know both how to be abased, and I know
how to abound: every where and in all things I am
instructed both to be full and to be hungry, both to
abound and to suffer need.*

—PHILLIPIANS 4:11-12

When we were dating, Ricardo and I used to talk all night about
all the things we loved, and music was always at the center of our
conversation. We were always passionate about music; it was one
of the commonalities that brought us together. We loved to share
new songs or artists we would hear on the radio or at the bookstore
with each other. In those days, we felt time was at our beck and
call, and we would do with it as we pleased.

Our lives were quickly changing into something that made
me feel uncomfortable and disconnected. Suddenly it seemed as
though life had taken an accelerated turn toward fulfilling the
ministerial and material needs, and the time we once wielded at
will, now began to betray us. The music that once united us now
seemed to be tearing us apart. Ricardo would spend many nights
in rehearsals and weekdays in preparation for the Sunday services,
and I felt left behind. He was passionate in his role as a worship
leader and embraced the speed at which things were moving, but
I couldn't keep up the pace. My days in the store seemed longer
than ever, and what at first was such a joy had now become a
heavy burden. The bookstore was supposed to be something we
both shared, but the responsibility had fallen squarely on my
shoulders, and I began to resent it. The customers' problems were
drowning me. On top of it all, communication between Ricardo
and I became a one-way street. He could hear me but wouldn't
listen. He was focused on his world—a world that was going
one hundred miles an hour—and I felt trapped in mine, one of
routines and boredom.

Ricardo and I began to drift apart, each one in our own world, without realizing the danger that was almost upon us.

My poor self-esteem also didn't help the situation. It was something that even as a little girl had affected me and always left me exposed to bad decisions. I recall one day Ricardo arrived at the bookstore to pick me up for church. He was running late and didn't notice at all that I had changed my hairstyle. It was a drastic change, and I expected some kind of reaction, even a simple, "You look great," or, "I love what you did with your hair." But there was nothing, as if I wasn't even there. To many wives, maybe this wouldn't have been a big deal. Some even get used to being ignored. But for me that moment was a game changer. I couldn't fully figure out why, but something inside me felt crushed, and it left me empty.

A lot of thoughts began to build up inside of me. The disillusion of not being able to get pregnant, the stress of the bookstore, the daily grind, and most of all, the lack of communication between Ricardo and I had been infiltrating my heart and affecting my emotions. The negative repercussions could no longer be ignored.

Now, I acknowledge and would agree with all who might say that such circumstances should never be an excuse to falter in life or to justify sin, but they are doors that, if left open, allow the enemy to put us in a vulnerable territory. That's where I found myself: fragile, frustrated, and with no exit strategy, trapped in a world that no longer appealed to me. I had abandoned prayer, and my relationship with God had become a passing one without any intimacy whatsoever. That in itself increased the profound emotional emptiness that led me to question whether or not He was actually listening.

SIN IS EXPOSED

There is an old proverb that says an idle mind is the devil's workshop. If you don't focus your mind on being productive, it is easy to fill it with sinful thoughts. I had lost sight of what was important, not appreciating what I had and looking to fill the void in my heart and my world with what I thought was missing. My desire was no longer to live according to God's purpose, nor to have my thoughts aligned with His Word and to look for guidance in prayer. Instead, I was entirely focused on—even consumed by—my disappointment with my life and marriage. It was there in that lonely place, far away from Him, that I began to make mistakes and bad decisions.

Without a doubt, the worst decision I ever made was done without much thought to or consideration of the repercussions it would have or the pain it would cause those who loved me the most. I broke the vow I had made to Ricardo four years earlier in front of God to be faithful till death do us part. When we married I had pronounced that vow with immense love and devotion, but I became a sinner without analyzing the damage I would bring to Ricardo's heart and our family. My selfishness had consumed me, pushing aside all I had learned as a child growing up in church. I simply believed it was what I needed and hoped it would fill the overwhelming void inside. I thought of only me and nothing else mattered.

Getting involved in a relationship outside of marriage immediately put on hold all of God's plans for my life, and I couldn't have felt further away from Him in that moment. I spent days in a cloud of confusion and desperation as a result of what I was doing. I wanted to end it, but I lived trapped in a sinful pit that I couldn't get out of. One lie led to another, and I found myself always trying to be one step ahead of the game. This wasn't a life worth living! I found it hard to sleep and began to suffer terrible nightmares. Nonetheless, nothing could compare to what awaited me in the coming months.

Not long after the affair began, I became so sickened by the situation I was in that keeping any food down was difficult, and I began to lose weight. Any loving gesture Ricardo made toward me would make me cry, something I learned to do only in the shower to continue the charade. I couldn't let him know that I was drowning in desperation.

My life in total disarray, I decided one day to turn away from my sin and end the relationship. I was going to concentrate on my marriage, keep my affair a secret from Ricardo, and leave this horrible episode behind me. At first I felt relief, but the weight of my sin was too much to bear, and it constantly tortured me, like a knife piercing my heart. That feeling of disgust with myself was always at the surface, and it didn't take much to make me feel like I was drowning in despair.

Overwhelmed with the burden of my actions, I decided to confide in a girlfriend of mine. She, feeling the matter was a delicate one with profound consequences, ended up sharing it with a leader from our church. I'll never forget the day he confronted me. As he entered through the doors of the bookstore I could see in his eyes how disappointed he was, and when he told me to close the doors my fears were confirmed. I began to cry, knowing full well what I had done. His words were merciless and harsh, like blades slicing up my heart. All that was hidden had been exposed, and in the full light of day it wasn't pretty. Feeling overcome by shame and disgust, I wanted the earth to open up and swallow me.

He began by saying, "I know what you've been doing," and without hesitation gave me two options: "Either you tell him, or I will." In the end, he was drawing his line in the sand. He told me to call my mother and confess to her what I had done, because apart from her I would have no one else by my side during this ordeal. He let me know that my best option would be to pick up my things, tell Ricardo I didn't love him and just leave. According to him, being young and not having children would make it easier for me to start a new life in another city or state far away. It was clear that in his eyes the hopelessness of our marriage didn't leave too many viable choices. But the words and advice he was giving me were final and void of hope. They weren't the same words I had read in the Bible or had heard in my father's sermons as a child. What about the woman at the well? Or the lost sheep? Where was the love of the father for the prodigal son? I had heard for so many years that God had the last word, but that wasn't what I was presented with in my moment of despair. I felt lost in a world of shame and confusion. The best way I can think of to describe my situation at the time was that of a stray dog; no sooner had I dirtied the carpet than I was kicked out of the house to fend for myself.

I called my mother in that very moment and told her everything that I had done. I could hear the pain in her voice as she said to me, "There is nothing impossible for God. Ask Him to forgive you and then ask Ricardo to forgive you. I know that he loves you."

I then called one of our employees to come and attend to the store since I couldn't stop crying and shaking, and I raced to my mom's house still dazed and confused. As I drove—I don't even know how—I begged God with every passing mile that my father wouldn't be home. To my great relief, he wasn't. I truly thought my mother would never want to see me again once I told her everything, but instead her embrace was desperate and strong, and in that moment I finally understood what she had always told me: "A mother's love flows deep in the soul. I will always love you no matter what. You are and will always be my daughter." She insisted I seek counseling and direction prior to making any long-term decisions. But in any case, she said, as hard and painful as it might be, confession was the only way to break the bondage of sin. She said she was sure that with God's help one day I would be able to lift my head up high again.

In the meantime, I was coming to grips with the fact that this self-inflicted wound was going to be more painful than anything I could ever have imagined. Acting foolishly and unwisely, I had thrown away all that which for so many years Ricardo and I had worked so hard to attain. Every vow I made on the day of our wedding—promising with heart and soul and with all sincerity never to break—was left worthless, laying on the floor in the face of all my actions. My words had no value, and once my sins were revealed to the public, everyone would have a thousand and one reasons to doubt me. I was damaged goods, tainted. My self-esteem was a problem before, but now my actions had left me feeling as though I were less than garbage. This profoundly affected me, and the thought of taking my life spread through every fiber of my body, nestling itself in my heart.

THE CONSEQUENCES OF SIN

The drive to my house seemed like an eternity, and I'd never seen my mother cry so much. Being so young and naive, my mind couldn't comprehend all that was going on, and it was overwhelming. I felt nauseated and had to stop to throw up.

All of a sudden it occurred to me: How could I confront Ricardo's family, who had been so amazing with me? How could I tell his mom, who had entrusted me with his heart? My mind was overwhelmed with questions and doubts.

The fear and sin inside me eclipsed everything I had been taught as child: that God is a God of forgiveness and restoration, of love and mercy. The only thing I could think of was how dirty and undesirable I was. The devil is a liar, and his main goal is to destroy—destroy your dreams, your marriage, and eventually your life. He ensnares you in sin, and for a while everything is good, till his true intentions are revealed.

Mired in the aftermath of my poor choices and totally overwhelmed, I flung my mom's car door open and started to throw myself out, but she managed to stop me just in time by quickly grabbing me by the arm. We cried together on the side of the road as she begged me not to do anything crazy, to please give God a chance. But in my mind there was no hope for me. I kept hearing a voice that whispered, "Take your life, for you are worthless." The hopelessness I felt was relentless.

Finally, we arrived at my house. Ricardo was already there waiting to leave to church that night, as he did every weeknight. He was totally unaware of the storm that was approaching his life, nor of the devastating pain that it would bring, breaking his heart in a thousand pieces. Nobody deserved the anguish he would be tasked to endure.

As I exited the car, my mother asked me if I loved him. Till that point no one had asked me that question. I knew without a doubt that I did.

On my way in the house a neighbor suddenly came out to say hello, an elderly lady who had always admired our young marriage, and I thought, What will she think of me now? My heart sunk deeper and for a moment my resolve slipped away. I stopped in front of my door and just stared at the lock. I could feel my blood pulsing in my ears. Fear had me paralyzed, but I knew this was something I could not run from, so I opened the door.

When I walked in, it was like I was seeing everything for the first time. It's amazing how clear things look when the veil of sin is lifted. The house, which not so long before seemed tired and old, had become the most beautiful mansion my eyes had ever seen. The secondhand furniture, the dilapidated stove, every simple decoration that Ricardo and I had collected throughout our four years of marriage were now invaluable. They all came back to life as if to remind me of their worth and how, because of my actions, I had thrown them all away. But in the end, the most painful moment was the realization that I had discarded the most wonderful and precious gift any woman could ever want: the love of a good man.

I had asked myself a thousand times, What went wrong? What changed in my heart? They were all valid questions with no worthy answers, and all I felt at that moment was immense remorse for the terrible pain I was about to inflict on my unsuspecting husband. I was sure he would want nothing to do with me and that my life was about to drastically change. I longed for his mercy, but knew I didn't deserve it. I tried desperately to memorize the photos on the wall and engrain the fragrance of our home in a secret place in my mind, somehow trying to make time stand still before it all slipped away, but as I heard him call out, "Babe, I'm in the office," I knew my time had run out.

I walked to the door, where I saw him sitting at his desk. I felt sick and started to tremble, but there would be no turning back. With a shake in my voice I said, "There's something I need to tell you." I asked him to sit on the sofa, and as I knelt before him with tears in my eyes and fear in my heart I spoke the words he never thought he would hear: "I've been unfaithful."

The Bible says in Proverbs 28:13, "He that covereth his sins shall not prosper: but whoso confesseth and forsaketh them shall have mercy". There would be no mercy for me that day. As Ricardo tried to make sense of what I'd just told him, his expression changed from confusion to pain and finally to full-out anger. When it all sunk in, he looked at me square in the eyes and said, "Give me your wallet." I obliged, after which he then proceeded to take out all of my credit and debit cards, returning just my driver's license and library card. I was left with zero financial support, and although it was painful, I felt I deserved it. My pain didn't matter much in that moment. The agony Ricardo must have felt as a result of my betrayal surpassed anything I could ever fathom. Right there and then, my selfish heart got a dose of reality, and I knew things would never be the same.

I had never seen anyone display so much anger and contempt. Ricardo's words were harsh, without filters or compassion, and aimed directly at my heart. When he was finished, he approached me on his knees with tears in his eyes and said, "I need for you to leave! When I get back I don't want you to be here. I never want to see you again!" He then got up, opened the front door, and walked out. I cried and screamed in vain, begging him not to leave, clinging to his legs and asking him to forgive me for what seemed to be a thousand times. But there weren't enough Forgive me's that night to ease his pain. His heart had quickly hardened, and the silent, icy stare he gave me said it all.

As he walked out, he found his friends waiting there to console him and take him away. They had been made aware of the situation by the church leader and were quick to come to his defense and give him much-needed support. As Ricardo and his friends drove away, I fell to my knees on the porch of our house and sobbed uncontrollably. I begged God to grant me some relief from the agony I had brought upon myself, the pain in my heart, and the unbearable weight of my sin.

I looked around to see if any of my friends had come for me, but I found myself alone. Besides my mother, no one came to intercede, to let me know everything would be OK or that God could somehow still work a miracle and fix this disastrous life of mine, restoring my marriage along the way. The cruel and painful reality, as I soon found out, was that my sin had made me wholly undesirable and easily disposable. The title of friend, sister, servant of God, and Ricardo's wife had little to no value at all in the hearts of those who had already found out about my indiscretions. My search to find words of encouragement and hope, prudent and wise counsel, or maybe someone to shed a little light and help me out of the dark nightmare I was living in went in vain.

To make matters worse, I still had to confront my father, the man who, from childhood, had raised me with Christian values, teaching me to honor God in everything I did. That night would turn out to be the longest and most painful one for everyone involved.

Once more hearing in my head that whispering voice telling me how worthless I was, I contemplated taking my life again. I remembered the rat poison we had in the garage and quickly went to retrieve it. I was frantic and desperate and just wanted to alleviate the excruciating pain and the feeling of hopelessness that had inundated every fiber of my being. With the box shaking in my hand and the tears streaming down my face, I asked God to forgive me. I told Ricardo I loved him from the bottom of my heart, wherever he was, and hoped one day he would forgive me for all the pain I'd caused. I then grabbed a handful of poison and went to put it in my mouth.

Suddenly, out of nowhere, the front door opened, and by the grace of God my mother walked in. Seeing the drama about to unfold before her, she immediately began to scream and cry. Throwing herself upon me, she fought to wrestle the poison from my hand. She yelled, "There is power in the blood of Jesus," over and over again and began to tell me how much I meant to her and how God truly loved me. Through her tears, she mentioned God's purpose for my life and how she knew one day I would see it come to pass.

But in that moment, all of that seemed impossible for me to believe. In the end, contemplating the anguish I was causing my poor mom just by nearly taking my life, I surrendered the poison and fell into her arms. We hugged for what seemed to be an eternity and soon after began the arduous task of packing all my belongings. It was one of the hardest things I've ever had to do in my life—that and finding the strength to continue living. I left my house that night with my world and my heart in pieces and all my belongings in garbage bags. Deep inside my broken heart I prayed that God would one day allow me to return home.

Chapter 3

THE POWER OF WORDS

by Susana Rodríguez

MY PARENTS' HOUSE was only five minutes from ours, and as we got closer, my mom whispered, "Leave your things in the car till we speak to your dad." It was obvious she was scared of what his reaction would be. So was I. As we entered, I felt a heavy weight on my shoulders. He was sitting in his favorite chair, and with heart in hand and head bowed I approached and sat beside him. Immediately he asked me for Ricardo, and again I began to cry. With a knot in my throat and a paralyzing shame, I once again pronounced those embarrassing and painful words: "Dad, I was unfaithful to him, and he threw me out of the house."

Once more, in the space of just a few hours, I experienced what it felt like to hurt another person I loved with the weight of my words. My father begged me to tell him that it was just a bad joke, that it wasn't true and everything was OK. But the nightmare was real—and only just beginning. The cruel reality of my sin had left another victim in its trail. My father, shocked and dismayed, couldn't understand what was happening and, falling to his knees, began to sob. I had never seen him cry that way before, and it shattered my soul.

After a few minutes had passed, he composed himself and asked me the grand question, "How could you do something like that to someone who loved you so much?" I didn't know what to say. His words were heart-wrenching, reinforcing my desire not to live. I didn't know how to console him, and the more he thought about what I had done, the more his anger grew. "How could you do that to our family?" he asked with pain and confusion. "What will our friends say? How are we going to face Ricardo's mother and grandmother?"

Sitting on the chair with tears rolling down my face, I felt smaller and smaller with every question he would ask. I couldn't take it anymore, and lifting my eyes towards the door, I bolted out. I wanted to disappear, but where could I go? I didn't have any money, nor transportation. I couldn't call anyone for fear of what they would say. So I walked back in to my parents' house and quickly locked myself in one of the bedrooms.

THE DARKEST NIGHT OF MY LIFE

My life had been so blessed. I had a husband, house, car, business, and everything any woman could want. Now, in an instant, it had all disappeared, and the sad and bitter reality of that fact had fallen over me like a bucket of ice cold water. Locked in that room I craved relief from the screaming voices inside my head and maybe just a little peace from the inevitable storm that awaited me outside that bedroom door. I needed to hear God's voice. I begged Him for a sign that all would be OK, some kind of assurance that I would live to see another day, but with every minute that passed all I could think of was a different way to end my life.

Sitting on the floor, I could hear my parents' conversation taking place on the other side of the door. My father had decided to go speak to Ricardo to try and convince him to forgive me and possibly give me another chance. He was desperate. I heard him tell my mother how just a few weeks earlier he had confronted a young girl in church who had been caught in adultery and had admonished her with no compassion or mercy. Now here he was dealing with a daughter who was also "a sinner, an adulterer!" What would people say? he asked.

My mother screamed at him, "Shut up! Can't you see that right now what people think or say doesn't matter? What matters is keeping her alive. She has no self-worth and feels like dying, and I'm really scared of losing our baby girl. We have to help her overcome this, because she has no one else but us at this moment."

Upon hearing those words I sank deeper into depression. I felt my body slowly shutting down and began to have what I can only explain as an out-of-body experience. I saw myself on the floor rocking back and forth in a fetal position, a pathetic excuse for a woman that wasn't even worth feeling sorry for. I hid underneath the bed and began to cry inconsolably. A thousand questions assaulted my mind. What's going to happen to me? Who am I? Could God still love someone like me? Why did I hurt the man I loved? Could he possibly forgive me one day?

That night was eternal. I cried and screamed in my pillow underneath the bed on that cold, hard tile floor till the sun came up. Why beneath the bed? Because it was the place I deserved. I didn't feel worthy of comfort, of a warm, soft bed and a blanket and pillow knowing that I had been the cause of so much pain. I could only think of Ricardo's face, full of disgust and rage, as he left our house surrounded by his friends. He hated me and wanted nothing to do with the woman he had chosen to be his wife four years earlier, the one whom he promised to protect and love in sickness and in health, till death did us part. But the painful truth was, I had broken that pact, that sacred vow we had made, with my selfish mistake. I was the one who destroyed the beauty of what we had. I understood too late that every action in life has its consequences, and that bitter pill was mine to swallow. Moving forward, the floor and I would become one. It was the lowest place for the dirtiest person. I felt so unworthy.

My mother would knock on the door constantly, but I wouldn't open. I didn't want to eat or drink, as even that felt like a privilege I didn't deserve. When she wasn't asking God to somehow comfort me in my hour of need, she would beg me not to do anything foolish and drastic. But there was no solace for me that night, nor any words of comfort from God in that desperate hour. There was only a silence that chipped away at my soul with every passing minute and reaffirmed to me that this crisis I had created would be my alone to confront.

I witnessed the sun set and then rise again from beneath that bed. At one point I exited the room to use the bathroom, hoping somehow my father would see me and I could feel his embrace once more, but it wasn't to be. My father's silence, along with my mother's constant pleas for me to eat, were too much for my fragile heart.

Words of Healing and Restoration

My mother, following the advice given to her, decided to send me to live with a high school friend of mine who was studying upstate approximately six hours north of Miami. But even there my silence and crying continued. I didn't eat and found refuge in the darkness the whole week I spent there. Finally, my friend, fearing for my life, asked my mother to please come pick me up. She had seen my condition and realized my life was in danger every minute I spent away from home. I was a lost soul bouncing from one place to the other like a yoyo. No one knew what to do with me.

No sooner had I returned to my mother's house than I went straight to the bedroom and hid underneath the bed again. My days and nights became one. I lost all notion of time going over and over in my head what I had done. I felt inundated by the painful words expressed to me by those who had once loved me and now so easily had tossed me aside. None of my girlfriends called me. No one from our circle of friends stopped by to see me or even to ask what had occurred. It was as if I ceased to exist. It was a very lonely time for me. I would sometimes ask my mother if Ricardo had called, knowing full well the answer would be no.

One day she passed a note underneath the door letting me know she would be stepping out for a bit to visit her doctor. By that time my headaches and stomachaches had gotten so bad I couldn't stand it anymore, so I stepped out of my room to search for something to eat, assuming no one would be there.

My eyes were swollen from crying all night, my mangled back in pain from sleeping on the floor, and my hair a full-blown, knotted mess. As I entered the kitchen I was surprised to see my father quietly sitting there at the table reading his Bible. He was just as shocked to see me and my appearance. I was no longer that beautiful girl he had raised and loved but was instead an unappealing, physical reminder of the ugly consequences of sin. Nevertheless, he asked me to sit with him, and there, without any notice, began to pray for me. His words transformed into heavenly tongues as his face was overwhelmed with tears. I knew for sure that God was there, and for the first time in a long time, I began to feel different. A warm sensation came over me, and although I couldn't understand what my father was saying, I knew those words were all about me.

He paused and told me that God had spoken to him and given him something special that I needed to hear. He then proceeded to open the Bible and read to me Jeremiah 15:19 (NIV):

> *Therefore this is what the Lord says: "If you repent, I will restore you that you may serve me; if you utter worthy, not worthless, words, you will be my spokesman. Let this people turn to you, but you must not turn to them."*

He stood up and took my hands, and speaking with a gentle voice, uttered the words I'd so longed to hear: "My daughter, I want you to know that I love you, and I will always love you. I am your father, and you are my daughter. Nothing you've done could ever change that. I'm sorry for not being there when you most needed me, but I promise from this day on, I will be with you every step of the way." We hugged for what seemed to be an eternity, and in that moment I felt not only my earthly father's embrace but also my heavenly Father's love and forgiveness. My father—who had been so angry and hurt that he couldn't even look at me—was now showing me love and assuring me I would no longer be alone to carry this burden of shame. It was more than my heart could take.

I couldn't believe what I was hearing, and I had him read the verse to me over and over again. It became my motto, the verse I would run to whenever I felt unworthy and ashamed. I understood in that moment that God still loved me and that there was hope for a new beginning if I allowed Him to transform my heart and my mind according to His will. I had to empty me of myself to allow God to completely fill me. That day marked a before-and-after in my life, and I wouldn't look back.

There aren't enough words to describe how I felt at that moment. All I can say is that it was as if I had been sinking to the bottom of the sea in the middle of a storm, and suddenly someone threw me a lifesaver to rescue me. My mind was racing to catch up with this revelation. Could this be real? Was I dreaming? Could my mind be playing tricks on me on account of me not eating? Was my heavenly Father really telling me He loved me through my earthly father? After everything I had done, was I truly being given another opportunity to start over?

My father's embrace in that moment was the sweetest and most loving one I had ever felt. He said, "Baby girl, the Bible is full of imperfect men and women who failed miserably in their lives, but they turned away from sin, and God restored them. King Manasseh, who at the age of twelve inherited the kingdom from his father, Ezequiel, spent a good portion of his rule being evil and unjust."

> *But Manasseh led Judah and the people of Jerusalem*
> *astray, so that they did more evil than the nations the*
> *Lord had destroyed before the Israelites. The Lord*

*spoke to Manasseh and his people, but they paid
no attention. So the Lord brought against them the
army commanders of the king of Assyria, who took
Manasseh prisoner, put a hook in his nose, bound
him with bronze shackles and took him to Babylon.
In his distress he sought the favor of the Lord his
God and humbled himself greatly before the God
of his ancestors. And when he prayed to him, the
Lord was moved by his entreaty and listened to his
plea; so he brought him back to Jerusalem and to
his kingdom. Then Manasseh knew that the Lord
is God.*

—2 CHRONICLES 33:9–13, NIV

My father continued to speak words that instilled life to
my fragile mind and tired soul. It was manna from heaven. He
explained, "King Manasseh represented everything that was evil
and angered God, disobeying his commandments every chance he
got. He sacrificed his children and caused so much pain. When
he was finally captured, in his moment of despair, he prayed to
God. Praying here represents asking for something in a formal and
anxious way. I'm sure he begged God with the last drop of strength
he had to save him from certain death."

That was exactly how I felt! I needed that anxious, desperate
prayer in my life. I needed God to hear me and see my contrite
heart.

Then my father told me God was able to forgive King Manasseh
and all the evil he had done to the point of restoring him. The Bible
says that in the end he was positioned as king once more. When
I heard this my heart was filled with hope—hope that one day I
too would be restored to my small kingdom, that the heart of my
heavenly Father would be moved by my humble prayers, and one
day I might have returned to me what I had lost on account of my
sin.

I think it was then that my father realized just how low I had become in my own eyes—so low that it took faith for me even to believe in the hope of grace someday. "How could God not forgive you?" my father asked. "How could I not forgive my only daughter? I am here to help restore you to a full and plentiful life in Jesus Christ, the life He originally intended for you." He then began to explain every verse that God had given him. I received it all with passion and hunger, remembering the first verse I memorized as a child.

As the deer pants for streams of water, so my soul pants for you, my God. My soul thirsts for God, for the living God. When can I go and meet with God? My tears have been my food day and night, while people say to me all day long, "Where is your God?"

—PSALM 42:1–3, NIV

There He was, with His words before me, and my father willing to explain them all with patience and love. That was the God who knew my name before I was born, the one who saw me marry and fail miserably, and even so, loved me unconditionally. He still loved Susana.

After that conversation with my father I ate something, and for the first time in weeks I retired to my room and slept on the bed. I fell asleep repeating Jeremiah 15:19–20 in my mind. I was tired, but my heart was hungry for all things God, the one I'd heard of all my life but hardly knew.

NEVER LOSE HOPE

It's important to understand—and I can't emphasize this enough—how great God's love is. It doesn't matter to what point sin, or the nature there of, has taken you; God always forgives and restores when there is true repentance and a contrite heart. I needed to hear that no sin could separate me from His love. That our God is a loving Father, always willing and able to forgive.

I'd love to tell you that my mental and emotional state had miraculously changed and everything was perfect, but truth is, it was still up and down and day to day. I was in the midst of a battle, and any energy I expended in the fight seemed to cost me dearly. It felt like for every two steps I took forward, the enemy pulled me one—or more—steps back. Nonetheless, I pressed on as well as I could with God's help and my parents'.

Several days after God spoke to my father, I received a call from Rachel, Ricardo's cousin. She and I had maintained a close relationship, and although she had been worried about me, she was fearful of what Ricardo would say if she ever reached out. Even so, risking his ire, she gave me a call. I recall the joy in my mother's voice when she knocked on the door to tell me Rachel was on the phone. I cautiously picked up the phone and said hello. She asked me how I was feeling, and I could only sigh. She knew this had not been easy on me. She also asked if I stilled loved Ricardo. I answered yes, to which she responded, "There is nothing impossible for God. Don't lose hope, although it may seem there is none. I'm praying for you."

I asked her about Ricardo, since I hadn't heard anything from him in weeks. She told me he hadn't been eating or sleeping much and was still very hurt and upset at me. She couldn't believe that none of our friends had called or come to visit, but she was happy I had answered her call and said she'd talk to me again soon. I hung up with a heavy heart, but at the same time I was thankful that someone had remembered me.

Later on that day my father and I sat down to read the Bible, like we'd been doing every day. All of a sudden we heard a knock at the door. It was one of Ricardo's friends. My heart was filled with joy to see a familiar face. I invited him in, and he sat at our table. He asked me how I'd been, but before I could even answer he revealed the true motive behind his visit. "Susi," he began with trepidation, "I'm here to serve you the divorce papers. Please sign them and don't make it harder than it already is for Ricardo."

I knew Ricardo wanted to divorce me. He had mentioned it in his moment of rage, but I never imagined it would happen so quickly, nor did I expect him to send a friend to serve me with the papers. Furthermore, the papers stated I was giving everything to Ricardo, everything we had worked so hard for during our marriage. I would be left with nothing—no house, no car, no business, but most of all, no Ricardo. I closed my eyes, and everything in me screamed, "Lord, are you there?" I ran into my room and hid in my safe place underneath the bed. I cried and prayed, knowing Ricardo's friend was waiting for my answer just outside the door. I didn't know what to do.

I cried out to God, "Lord, I've turned my back on sin. I've asked for forgiveness! Please, Lord, please, what should I do?" All of a sudden Jeremiah 15:19 came to mind, and I was filled with an overwhelming peace. In that moment I knew God would restore everything the enemy had stolen. I knew it would be a difficult, if not impossible, task, but I was no longer alone and no longer afraid.

I came out of the room and headed straight over to where Ricardo's friend was impatiently waiting. I sat down and said within me, "Lord, I trust in You." And with a flick of the wrist I signed away all material belongings I ever owned, with the exception of the clothes that were still in garbage bags spread throughout my mom's house. I returned to my room and knelt down crying as I prayed, "Jesus, I need You. Don't forget me. I know that I'm broken, but You can restore me. I might not be worth much, but I'm willing to do what You want. Don't forget me." I had little energy left that day, but the new hope that had risen within me rekindled my resolve to keep moving forward toward restoration, no matter how long it would take.

A few days had passed since the signing of the divorce papers when another surprise visitor came by the house. This time it was a friend who had worked with the youth in the church. He sat with me in my parents' living room and asked me how I was doing. He mentioned his father's infidelity and the pain it had caused his family. But his words were uplifting and full of hope, and I could sense the sincere worry he felt in his heart for me. He told me he and his wife had been praying for my life and offered their support in whatever I needed. It felt great to talk to someone other than my parents, and it did me good. He'll never know how much that visit meant to me and how God used him at the perfect time to nudge me forward in my journey.

FINDING STRENGTH IN HIS WORD

My prayer life was my source of strength, and I felt Jesus beside me at every moment. I would visit a local park with my father every day trying to exercise my legs since most of the time I was on my knees in prayer and they were beginning to hurt. I started with one mile, which turned into three and, finally, six miles a day. My father would sit under a tree watching me walk as I spoke to my friend, Jesus. It did me good to be outside with the sun, the trees, and all of God's beautiful creations. I enjoyed my daily walks with my father, my companion, always close by, watching me grow every step of the way.

Ever since Ricardo's friend served me the divorce papers, my parents and I had officially declared war on anything that would come between me and the restoration of my marriage. Even in spite of my walking, I had calluses on my knees from spending so much time kneeling in prayer, but I didn't care. I had one goal and God's promises before me!

When I wasn't praying at home, my mother and I would go for short drives to engage in spiritual warfare from my parents' car. Ricardo's house was less than a mile from my parents', so my mom and I began to drive by late at night, when he was sleeping, to pray for my home and Ricardo's heart.

His Word sustained me, and along with His presence, it was all I ever desired. I would wake up very early, at sunrise, in search of God's face and asking Him to fill me with His strength. I would continuously listen to worship music in my room, and I had my favorite songs on repeat all day long, driving my parents nuts, though they understood I needed every bit of positive influence I could get just to help me through the day. I was still weak in spirit and mind, and if I didn't feel His presence in my life at any moment, fear would engulf me. Any news, as insignificant as it might be, could break me.

Ricardo's lawyer had sent some papers with a court date to finalize the divorce, bringing a sad and painful end to our marriage. The day arrived, and like always, I woke up early to pray and spend time with God. I got dressed and left with my mom to go to downtown Miami, where the court was. We got a little lost and had a hard time finding parking, which caused us to arrive late to the proceeding.

I walked into an elevator, and there I saw Ricardo for the first time in a long time. My heart was beating a mile a minute. I wanted to run into his arms and hug him—the man that I loved, with whom I had shared so many laughs and tears, and who's heart I had destroyed. He looked thin and different standing there next to his lawyer. As my mom and I approached them, his lawyer turned to him and said, "You don't have to talk to her or even look at her." Her words were cold and cruel, and I thought, "This woman barely knows me."

Before Ricardo walked out of the elevator he just said, "You didn't have to come. It's just a formality." I never got the memo. It was a painful and humiliating moment that could've been avoided, but God's plans are not ours. I said I was sorry, turned around, and walked down the court stairs, my face drenched in tears. I wanted to scream from the immense pain I felt, but I held it in and whispered to God, "Lord, I know You are with me, and I trust You."

HIS BIRTHDAY

Ricardo's birthday was approaching, and I wanted to give him something special. I didn't have money, so I decided to bake him some cookies. On the day of his birthday I placed them in a small box and decorated it with a blue bow. I looked in my garbage bags for something nice to wear and fixed my hair up in a different way to try and look pretty for him. I asked my mom to drive to his house and wait in the car for me.

I found the courage to walk up to the door, not staying at a distance, like I usually did when I would come at night to pray. As I approached I could see next to the door at least six boxes addressed to Ricardo, in all different shapes and sizes, with beautiful ribbons and bows. One of them said, "To Ricardo, my favorite singer." It was from a friend of mine from church. I couldn't believe it. Reading the rest, I realized they were all from girls we knew in church. I was angry but most of all hurt. There they were, the girls I thought were my friends, whom I patiently waited for and longed to hear from in my moment of need, making a move on the man who just a month earlier was my husband. I suddenly understood why the calls never came; they were too busy making a beeline to win over Ricardo's heart. They didn't care that he was still hurting and his heart was in pieces, and they surely didn't think twice about how I was feeling.

Then I thought, what right did I have to question anyone after all that I'd done? I was the one who broke his heart, and it was because of me that he was now free to do as he pleased. My opinion on the matter was insignificant and held no merit. I had lost all rights to Ricardo.

I knocked on the door, fearing what he would say. Would I hear the harsh words full of loathing and anger? Would I be able to stand there and take them like before? Fear overtook me, and I decided to leave my gift box along with the others and return to the car where my mother had been waiting. When I got to the gate

I heard Ricardo open the door and say, "Hey, what's up?" I turned around and responded, "I just wanted to come by and wish you a happy birthday. I brought you some cookies I baked. I really hope you like them."

He looked at the box, and then looked at me and rolled his eyes. He was so angry he couldn't hide it. My heart sank.

"I won't bother you anymore," I said. "I just wanted to try and make your day special."

Then I thought, "Make his day special? How can I make his day special if I'm the reason it's so miserable?" It was my fault and my fault alone he was so hurt. Looking in his eyes, there was no denying the pain he was feeling. It was obvious, and it made me feel like a fool. Seeing my small gesture surrounded by the balloons and flowers he'd already received just made matters worse. I felt that familiar knot in my throat and turned around to leave when I heard him ask, "How've you been?"

"Alright, I guess," I answered.

"You look different, very skinny."

"Yes," I said. "You too."

I couldn't contain my tears and slowly walked away. He quickly closed the door, and just like that, he was gone.

My mind was swimming. "How did I get here? How could I have lost this man that once loved me so much? Why didn't I value our friendship and all the beautiful things we once shared?" We had so much in common and always enjoyed being in each other's company. We planned to one day travel the world and even dreamed of having kids, two of them. We wanted to grow old together, but instead, just wound up growing apart.

BACK TO SQUARE ONE

My father noticed how much my visiting Ricardo had negatively affected me, opening up wounds and pushing me back into a depressive state, and he understood that since my strength was gone it was up to him and my mom to keep me afloat. They prayed and read the Bible with me, always trying their best to give me love and support. My wonderful mother would always prepare me my favorite meals, and although I wasn't very hungry most of the time, I did my best not to disappoint her. I tried to be more positive around them, seeing how difficult it had been on their busy schedules—each with their own lives yet at the same time carrying the weight of my mistakes. It couldn't have been easy.

I knew I had to put in maximum effort if the battle was to be won, but in all honesty, at times it seemed like a lost cause. It the midst of everything I still fought to find rest, but my mind wouldn't let me. The same questions and accusations would crawl back into my head time and time again, driving me insane. "How could you have done such a thing? Look at the disaster you've created. You're just a worthless sinner." Those questions would always take me down a spiral of anguish and desperation, straight to the same, familiar place in my room.

I knew it didn't matter how many times I would ask Ricardo to forgive me or tell my family how sorry I was; it would never be enough to make up for all I'd done. I understood it would take more than words and promises to win back their trust and their love. I would have to show them how sorry I was by living a life worthy of a second chance. There weren't any guarantees, nor promises of reconciliation, but I knew there was nothing impossible for God.

Chapter 4

GOD IS FAITHFUL

by Ricardo Rodríguez

THAT'S HOW IT ALL FELL APART—as if an atomic bomb had fallen on our house without warning, destroying in seconds what for years we had struggled to build. That fairytale dream we had just been living, in an instant had turned into ashes and debris and one horrible nightmare. All that I valued and of which I felt so proud had now become part of the most embarrassing chapter of my life.

Who was this woman before me on her knees asking me to forgive her? I didn't recognize her. The things she was confessing to me couldn't be real. I could feel my face changing, my stomach churning. I felt sick when I heard those words, the ones I thought I'd never hear.

I wish I could tell you my reaction was that of an honorable Christian man, compassionate and full of forgiveness. That I embraced her and told her everything would be alright. But truth be told, in that moment, as much as I tried to fight it, I couldn't contain my rage. The reins of fury and anger were released, and an unrelenting storm of verbal and emotional abuse fell upon Susana till my strength gave out. In fact, it took every bit of self-control I could muster just so I wouldn't physically assault her. But my words—my words had no mercy, and I hit her with everything I had. I wanted to make her feel as bad as, if not worse than, what I was feeling at the moment, and I succeeded by showering her with contempt and humiliation, with those words reserved only for your worst enemies, the ones you detest with such passion you wish they'd fall off the face of the earth. That was my reaction.

She continued begging me, still on her knees and with tears rolling down her cheeks, to forgive her. Over and over again she cried, "Forgive me. Forgive me." But I wanted nothing to do with forgiveness and even less to do with her in that moment.

CRISIS AND CHARACTER

I thought I was a good man, and looking back I probably was. I served God with a sincere heart and considered myself a good friend, an exemplary son, and a faithful husband. I had all the qualities to succeed in life and find happiness. Therefore, the words that my wife was uttering to me in that moment didn't make any sense. How could this be happening to me? I'd always been of strong character, fearless under difficult circumstances, and was rarely overwhelmed by life's pitfalls. I thought I knew it all and that nothing or no one could bring me to my knees, but this was so different.

In life, it's the fiery trials that refine us, separating the precious metals from the ore, and ultimately revealing our true character. I always saw myself as being made of solid gold, but in that moment the real Ricardo was revealed, and he was closer to the Tin Man than anything else. I quickly realized I had control of nothing— not my wife's actions, not the reactions of those who would soon find out all that she had done, nor, even less, control over my own emotions. Those same emotions that I had fought so hard to hide throughout my life were now being exposed for the world to see. They, too, were betraying me.

I had always been the one who always gave the sound advice, the friend with the calm and collected demeanor who could be trusted and relied on. And yet I found myself, the man of faith whose trust in God had no rival and was always willing to courageously face whatever storms life might bring, suddenly doubting, broken, and afraid. Oh, but how things change when it's you that has to walk through the fire. D. L. Moody says, "Character is what you are in the dark."[1]

In the Bible we see Daniel's true character showing up when, even though his life was in the balance, he decided not to contaminate himself with the king's food and wine. Once again in the lion's den, facing certain death, he never wavered under insurmountable odds. In those crucial moments of his life, his true character was revealed. In the same way, Abraham, Moses, Joseph, David, Ruth, Peter, Paul, and so many other great men and women of God found their places in the history of our faith because in the storm, when all seemed lost and they could've easily given in or given up, instead they rose to their knees, displaying their unwavering trust and faith in an almighty God for all to see.

Your true character is revealed when you are confronted by situations that take you beyond your limits, past your capabilities, and out of the reach of your understanding. The truth is, who you are only shows up in the impossible, painful, and incomprehensible circumstances of your life. They are life's exams, which always come to define and unmask. Till that moment, my life had been one of blessing and favor, praise and applause, never having to experience the level of pain, confusion, and chaos I was now confronting. I was being taken out of my comfort zone, and my true self was finally coming to light.

I had been unmasked that night, like Susi, but in contrast to her, my temperamental and spiritual shortcomings were approved and expected. No one dared confront me that night about how little of Christ's character I was reflecting in such a life-defining moment. There was no mention to me of love, mercy, compassion, or restoration, though, it fact, it was then I needed to hear it the most. I was given *carte blanche*, and I took it and ran.

Pressure, conflict and chaos don't define your character; they only bring forth what is already there. The character of the believer is molded daily by the presence of the Holy Spirit in his life. The Bible says:

But the fruit of the Spirit is love, joy, peace, longsuffering, gentleness, goodness, faith, meekness, temperance: against such there is no law.

—GALATIANS 5:22–23

IT ALL CAME CRASHING DOWN

I learned that night, to my surprise, that my faith had its limits, that my strength wasn't what I thought it was, and that my character definitely wasn't like Jesus's. Susi had confessed her sins, and by doing so exposed her faults for all the world to criticize and shame. I hadn't confessed anything but had also been exposed before God as a fraud and a charlatan with my reaction. I didn't acknowledge it at the time, but there it was, plain as day for all to see. My words and actions in that defining moment shined a light on the shallowness of my relationship with Christ, and my unwillingness to show restraint or consider patience and prayer as viable options in the midst of that horrible storm showed everyone, including myself, what I was really made of.

Where was the love I'd sang of so many times? Where was the mercy and compassion when Susi needed it the most? What about the forgiveness and grace bestowed to me on the cross that I had so willingly accepted? Why was it so hard for me now to pass it on? These were issues that later on God would have to address in my own life. But in that moment there was no remedy for the disaster that was our marriage.

I grabbed her purse and proceeded to take out all of her credit and debit cards, leaving her with just her license and a library card. I revoked her dignity and whatever authority she had earned throughout our marriage. When I was done I told her I never wanted to see her again!

I tried to process all the information I'd just been given, but my mind raced out of control. As I made my way out of the house, her mother cried out, "Please have mercy!" but I couldn't muster up an ounce of mercy that night. Being greeted by my friends outside the door, I quickly left. It was all too much for me to take.

Hours later, when I returned, the drama continued. Susi was still in tears as she and her mother put all her belongings in garbage bags. I stood by and hurried her up without any concern or sympathy. It was a terribly sad scene, and trying to find the words to describe it proves difficult. All I can say is, I was caught up a mixture of agony, fury, shame, humiliation, and vengeance. There were tears, pain, and anger like I'd never experienced, and for sure those who witnessed it would say the same. Susi was in agony after seeing all the destruction and pain her sin had put in motion, I was choking on the bitter pill of her betrayal, and all others present seemed not to know what to do. I know for my mother-in-law it was especially painful, seeing as her daughter was at the epicenter of such a powerful storm of blame and judgment and sensing how the multitude was quickly gathering around her with stones in hand. I could see in her face the anguish she was feeling and her desperate desire to somehow find a fix for the situation. But there would be no relief, nor any fixing the damage that had been caused.

I was cruel and unjust, and I crossed the line. I went far beyond what Susi deserved, not realizing she too was suffering—had been suffering—with the shame and disdain that those who found out what she had done were just now beginning to display. But I hated being the victim, and I wanted payback.

Years later, as I reflected on how it all went down that night, it crossed my mind that no one ever said to me, "Take it slowly. Tomorrow is another day. Don't make any long-term decisions in a moment of crisis." Perhaps that was because of the sensitive nature of the matter or the fact that my anger was out of control. Nevertheless, it would've been nice to hear a measured and calming voice, along with some wise counsel, at such an important crossroads in my life.

As Susi walked out of our house for the last time, the painful reality began to set in. I tried to show strength and resilience in front of my friends, but in reality inside I was destroyed, feeling like a hurting child in need of someone to hug and acting as such. Here was the woman I had planned to spend the rest of my life with walking out with all her belongings in garbage bags, stripped of all authority and deprived of her dignity. I had used hostility and contempt as my shield and sword and embraced bitterness and anger as you would a best friend. But that painful night when I finally saw her leave and I was left in my loneliness to ponder all that had transpired, none of that could save me from feeling defenseless and vulnerable, doubting myself and all those around me, and finally, questioning God.

LESSONS LEARNED

Every crisis and storm we face in our lives is always a great opportunity for God to be glorified. These situations are authorized exams given to showcase what we've learned and where we stand in relation to Him. Sometimes we see them coming, but most of them, especially the truly difficult ones, arrive unannounced. That night would've been a great moment for God to be lifted high. Had I allowed it, it was another opportunity for Him to demonstrate His healing and redeeming power over a marriage that had been left for dead. I can only imagine God looking down from heaven, arms crossed, and saying, "I'm waiting on you to be the man I know you can be and do what you know is right." I can visualize all the wonderful things He had prepared for us that night—and how sad and disappointed He must have felt seeing my reaction and my lack of character.

Our story had a happy ending, but we could've avoided so much pain if I had just been obedient and applied some of those basic principles of love and forgiveness I had been taught as a child. Although the catalyst of all that took place that night had been my wife's sin, I had many opportunities to open up my heart and allow something supernatural to occur. That's how it is with every tragedy we face in life. Each and every one of them, as difficult and hard to comprehend as they might be, represent a great opportunity for God to display His power and ultimately be glorified in an amazing way. In fact, I guarantee you, if you look back you'll find dozens of times in your life in which God wanted to show Himself strong in the midst of your failures and mistakes but simply wasn't given the chance. You decided instead to hang on to the anger and bitterness, the hate and resentment. Maybe guilt, low self-esteem, or self-hatred have been stumbling blocks on your path toward God's perfect destiny and ultimate purpose for your life. The road that follows God's will for us is not always the easiest, but it is always the most rewarding. There will always be more opportunities when we find ourselves failing some of life's exams, but wouldn't it be great if at every turn and every chance, we would take the time to let God be God and allow Him to work His miracle in our shattered lives?

I had to acknowledge with time that I wasn't who I pretended to be and that I would never reach the grandeur of God's perfect plan without first living a life according to Christ. I had to accept the process and allow my mind and my heart to be made new if ever God was going to glorify Himself in my failures.

First Days

Those first days after everything came to light were sad and dark. I didn't want to tell my mother or grandmother anything, seeing as it would affect my grandma's health and my mother's heart. They loved Susi dearly, and I knew that it would be incredibly difficult for them to hear what she had done. When I finally spoke to my mother, detailing all that had occurred, she looked at me and asked, "How is Susi doing? Where is she? Can I talk to her?" This surprised me. I didn't expect such common-sense, ordinary questions in such a tumultuous situation. But her reaction, or lack thereof, gave me peace, something I'd been longing for.

I had forgotten that my mother had already experienced tragedy with the death of my father when she was young. She had dealt with grief and loss and could testify about God's faithfulness with authority and conviction. Her faith had been tested, and she had passed with flying colors. She spoke to me calmly and gave me words of hope, displaying what I was lacking: the character of Christ. She was the first person who didn't panic but instead brought peace and strength to the storm that was my life. She spoke to me as a mother but also as a woman of God, depositing words of wisdom and healing in my broken heart. She told me she would visit Susi as soon as she could and not to worry, that everything would be OK.

My grandmother's reaction was different. I couldn't tell her; it was too difficult. In turn, my mother spoke to her and filled her in on what transpired. Grandma and I never spoke about the matter, but she did what she would always do ever since I was child when facing giants and mountains: she prayed. She was a prayer warrior who won her greatest battles on her knees. This too gave me peace, knowing a least I had two precious women of God praying for me.

Having to carry the shame and stigma that being a victim of infidelity brings wasn't easy. I recall that first Sunday after everything came to light. As I entered through the front doors of the church I felt paralyzed by fear. In my mind, everyone knew what happened, and their sympathetic stares were too much to bear. I felt very unsure, and my walk reflected it. I was living a nightmare I couldn't wake up from, and with every step I took my smile became harder to fake. I realized the world wasn't stopping for me, that even those who not so long before had advised divorce had now continued on with their respective lives like nothing had happened, while mine was still in shambles. Everyone was back in their daily routines, but I couldn't figure out how. I wanted everyone to feel what I was feeling. I wanted the earth to take a break from spinning while I got my life back together. But that was never to be, and the loneliness was overwhelming.

The one thing that did help me push back depression and suppress the pain, if only for a while, was leading worship on Sunday mornings. It was my refuge. Being able to lift my voice and praise God in the storm was an oasis in my desert of misery. It was where I forgot my grief and found relief from the constant torment, and I could escape the grim reality of the life that awaited me when I got home. We had five services, and I was in charge of leading worship in each one. It was in those first services back that I learned the true meaning of worship, as I struggled to get through every song. I understood that God was still worthy, although He was silent, that the circumstances surrounding me could never take away from who He was. He was the one true, living God, the great I am, my Provider, and my Deliverer.

It was all part of the process, and even today I consider it the moment I finally became a true worshiper. When I lifted my voice in praise I remembered His promises for me, His faithfulness in past trials, and the mercy and grace He had always shown me the many times I had undoubtedly failed Him. In front of the multitude the world disappeared, and I found a hiding place.

But when it all finished and everyone said their good-byes, it would all come crashing down. As soon as I would get in my car and start my drive home, the waves of despair and anxiety would begin to swell, and the bitterness and rage would once again overtake me. My wounded heart couldn't handle the memory of Susi's betrayal, and with each passing day, it would get worse. I was resolute on ending everything and wanted nothing to do with reconciliation. Even so, there was always an internal struggle that would rob me of my peace and would leave me wondering, "Maybe..."

LONG-TERM DECISIONS FOR
SHORT-TERM PROBLEMS

The divorce process was quick. In the end, Susi bowed to my demands, keeping nothing more than her maiden name. She gave me the house, the car, the business, and retained no financial support. I remember the day I had to stand before the judge and verbally tell her that our marriage couldn't be salvaged. She asked if we had exhausted every resource and made every effort possible to find a solution for whatever ailed our marriage. She wanted to know if I was sure of the decision I was about to make and asked me one more time to verbally approve it. I responded with a simple yes, and as I said it I felt a profound sadness deep inside of me, the kind you only feel when someone you love has died. In less than two months everything was finalized, and we were divorced.

I figured with the divorce out of the way I would find relief and a bit of peace in my life. I assumed with a brand-new day and that bitter chapter of my life being closed, all would be OK. I was wrong. The following months were the worst of my life, a season of pain I wouldn't wish on anyone. The days were long and extremely sad and lonely. I lost thirty pounds in just thirty days, a diet I wouldn't recommend.

I continued with my responsibilities in church as worship leader, and although it wasn't easy, I never wavered. Those were still the only moments I could find a break from the pain. But through it all I longed for someone to throw me an anchor in this sea of despair I was still drowning in, someone with a word of encouragement and hope who would say, "Don't give up. There's still a chance. There is nothing impossible for God."

One day while I was tending to the bookstore, a local pastor by the name of Julio Landa stopped by and introduced himself. He told me my mother-in-law had spoken to him and explained our situation, and he said that as he was praying for us God prompted him to come and speak to me. He asked if I had a few minutes to spare, and in spite of feeling a bit defensive I reluctantly said OK. I closed the bookstore, and as we sat down on some chairs in the back he began to speak. I was skeptical at first, still feeling hurt and vulnerable, but there was something inside me that said, "Just sit and listen." As soon as he began to talk, a peace came over me, and I knew without a doubt this was a godly visit.

He asked me if I stilled loved Susi, or if any positive emotions remained in my heart toward her. He then asked if I believed in miracles. The answers to all those questions were the same: yes, but with some conditions. Susi and I were already divorced, and I didn't see any hope in reconciliation. I personally hadn't heard of anyone remarrying the same person after divorce, but I opened my heart, and he continued to speak.

He said, "God brought me here to tell you this: Marriage is like a garden. From the moment you say, 'I do,' you begin working the soil. You start by taking out the stones and debris that represent problems in each other's characters, you clean out the weeds that can become a hindrance to good communication, and with time, you start to see a beautiful garden bloom right before your eyes, a garden full of trust, love, hope, and dreams.

"One day, as it often happens in life, just when you are enjoying the beauty of your garden as it blooms in glorious splendor, disaster strikes, and a great fire burns everything to ashes. Your dreams, your hopes, and your trust are gone before you even realize what happened. My question to you is, Would it be better to leave that soil in its burnt state and start brand new somewhere else, or to once again try and salvage what appears to be unsalvageable? God tells you this: 'Underneath that burnt soil there is still fertile ground. If you embrace forgiveness and reconciliation, I will make that garden bloom like never before. It will surpass even your wildest dreams, for I will glorify myself in your failures, and all the world will see that I am the God of restoration.'

"You have the power in your hands to bless or to curse Susana's life. No one else can position her in her rightful place. God has forgiven her, and her salvation is not in the balance, but only you can grant her the blessing of once again being called Ricardo's wife. The decision is yours alone and cannot be delegated."

Like an arrow straight to the heart, his words hit their mark. Did I do the right thing in divorcing Susi? Should I have looked for better counsel and not jumped the gun as I did? The more I pondered his analogy, the more doubt kept creeping in. But how could I turn back time and change the past? It still seemed like such an impossible miracle that my mind just couldn't comprehend the possibility of reconciliation.

As I look back now on Pastor Landa's visit that day, I can clearly see God's hand preparing the soil in my heart for what was to come. Pastor Landa's words planted a seed of hope, and that seed would soon bloom into a supernatural miracle that forever transformed my life. He didn't know me and had nothing to gain by taking time out of his busy schedule to counsel me; he was just an obedient servant brave enough to speak to the broken heart of an angry young man. But oh, what a difference it made in my life.

INTERNAL CONFLICTS

It's important to recognize that we serve a God of action and not reaction. He is the Great I am who always has everything under control. He is the God who had everything in your life planned to perfection since before the foundation of the world. So keep in mind that even when you stray from the original plan and all seems lost, even when the solution escapes you and your hope is gone, He has already put a plan of salvation in motion for you. His world is not one of coincidences; in fact, He is the most excellent of designers, the supreme architect, and meticulous to perfection. There is always a contingency plan if you know where to look.

In those first weeks I can't recall the amount of times I got home after closing the bookstore not remembering how I even made it. My mind and emotions were constantly clouded, and I was still living in a state of shock. I'm positive whatever I managed to do in those days was done with the help of divine intervention. For sure I wasn't in any condition to do much of anything. Divorce can best be described as the death of a loved one without the actual, physical loss, and I was mourning the loss of my friend and the dreams we shared.

Throughout the years I've had friends who've privately shared with me their intimate feelings toward other women who weren't their wives. They've mentioned how good those women have made them feel, how well they got along, and the temptation they struggled with every time they communicated. I'm always astonished as to how they enter these dangerous relationships without ever thinking of the consequences, so easily forgetting the victims who, sooner or later, would have to pay for their mistakes. Every time I hear about one of these relationships I'm transported to that painful scene in my home office, seeing my wife once again on her knees begging me for forgiveness. I'm reminded of the terrible suffering she went through and the profound pain she brought to my heart, leaving it shattered. I've seen the terrible price of sin, and my response to those thoughts is always the same: it's not worth it. Sin destroys, uprooting all hope and leaving deep scars in the hearts of both the guilty and the innocent. Infidelity is portrayed as such an innocuous and painless action in the movies, without consequences or repercussions. But the reality is so different, and unfortunately you only find out when it's too late.

Marriage is a godly institution; it's not only a legal union but a spiritual and emotional one. The Bible says in Mark 10:8–9 (niv): "'And the two will become one flesh.' So they are no longer two, but one flesh. Therefore what God has joined together, let no one separate." This passage is referring to something supernatural, a heavenly union not made to be broken. That's why it hurts so much, that's why there will always be trauma and internal conflict whenever divorce is contemplated. If I only had a time machine and were able to take my friends back to relive those first months of anguish and despair right after my divorce. If they could walk a mile in my shoes through that ocean of pain—where you struggle to find sleep at night and the mornings bring no relief, where you lose the desire to eat and struggle just to breathe and at the turn of every corner is a reminder of what used to be—I'm sure they would think twice.

My advice for those friends is based on personal experience and what the Bible says in Ezekiel 18:30: *"Therefore I will judge you, O house of Israel, every one according to his ways, saith the Lord God. Repent, and turn yourselves from all your transgressions; so iniquity shall not be your ruin."*

YOUR MIRACLE IS AWAITING YOUR REPENTANCE

Weeks went by without any word from Susi. There wasn't much desire on my part to communicate, but she always made the effort. She would subtly leave notes on the door, and every once in a while I would see her slowly drive by our street with her mom. A couple of months after it all exploded and on the day of my birthday, she came by bearing some cookies she had lovingly baked. She had no money or employment, and it was all she could offer. But once again, embracing the anger and bitterness, I treated her with contempt and resentment. It was something I had gotten used to doing, though it was becoming more and more difficult to apply.

Susana had confessed her sin. She had repented and turned her back on her immoral ways, and God was going to glorify Himself in her life in spite of me. Without me knowing, she had also begun a spiritual battle on her knees for her marriage.

I didn't have much interaction with my friends either during that time. Some I avoided. The rest disappeared on their own account. I don't blame them. It was a very uncomfortable and embarrassing situation for most. You had to truly want to suffer if you approached me in that period of time. Other than my mother, I had no one to open up to and share my burden.

But there are always exceptions to every rule, and my exception's name was Rachel, my cousin on my father's side. We grew up together and had cultivated an appreciation for each other and a respectful and longstanding friendship. But in all honesty during that time, more than a friend, she had become a painful thorn in my side. She was the only one who wasn't afraid to tell me what I needed to hear and not so much what I wanted to hear. Although she was sympathetic about my suffering and loss, she wasn't about to let me drown in my sorrow, nor live there forever. We had many discussions—or better yet, arguments—in which she would confront me about my lack of compassion and forgiveness, always letting me know it was never too late to start over. Every time I felt the need to remind her of all that Susi had done, she would remind me of everything Jesus had done for me on the cross. When I would mention that I had the right to do what I wanted to based on what the Bible said, she would just say, "Grace and mercy always trump justice and law." She was relentless, always praying for a miracle.

Rachel was one of the few people who never stopped communicating with Susi. In fact, she was there in some of the worst moments of her life, always encouraging her to not to give up the fight. When all others were running away from the fray, she fearlessly dove in, sometimes confronting criticism from family members and constantly being pelted by my anger. That is the nature of a true friend: bold and honest, of Christlike character, obedient to God's voice, and unafraid to embrace, regardless of the consequences, what for sure they know is the right thing to do.

God used my cousin Rachel as a shining light to help me find my way out of that dark world that had taken control of my heart. In retrospect, I can see that God, with His contingency plan, had begun to put together a group of people who were fighting on His behalf to prepare the soil for the supernatural miracle that was to come. All that was needed were my obedience and forgiveness.

Chapter 5

BROKENNESS AND ANOINTING

by Ricardo Rodríguez

FOR YEARS I used the phrase "You don't know what I've been through" strategically to avoid any potentially profound or embarrassing conversations that might cause me to relive the shame of that terrible chapter in my life. Furthermore, I assumed no one actually wanted an honest answer to any questions about how I was really doing. I reasoned that if I took the time to tell them, they probably wouldn't appreciate having me unload on them emotionally, and I'd just end up wasting both my time and theirs. Now, I very much understand that superficial generalizations are not enough. I believe it's of the utmost importance to speak frankly and with transparency about the failures and errors in our lives, if only for the sake of saving one person from repeating those same mistakes. To talk about painful and embarrassing moments of our past requires genuine conviction, and Susi and I do it with the clear knowledge that it is only for one purpose: to share lessons learned and pitfalls to be avoided, to bring the hope of restoration where there once was none, and to invite the possibility of healing through the power of forgiveness. Our sincere motivation, beyond anything else, is to let it be known without a doubt that sin deceives and destroys, eventually condemning all who fall into its trap to physical, emotional, and financial ruin. However, the love of God, along with repentance and forgiveness, can lift you up from the lowest of the lows so that you can, once again, find joy and peace within His perfect plan.

71

It's important that each of us understands that the impossibly difficult struggles of our lives are necessary, and that each one of them represents another opportunity for God to glorify Himself and for our spirits to be strengthened. All those who wish to ascend to the heights of the great men and women of God we read of in the Bible will have to be bent, broken, and made anew, with the sole purpose of being perfected and elevated to a greater understanding of the Father's heart. This elevation is not in fame or fortune but in the powerful anointing only the Holy Spirit can provide—the anointing that in a supernatural way can lift a desperate and shattered heart out of the miry clay, fill it with hope and faith, and set it upon the solid rock. It is this anointing that instills the wondrous, transformative power of God's grace and mercy into the lives of the lost and the hopeless.

> *Brothers and sisters, I do not consider myself yet to have taken hold of it. But one thing I do: Forgetting what is behind and straining toward what is ahead, I press on toward the goal to win the prize for which God has called me heavenward in Christ Jesus.*

> —PHILIPPIANS 3:13–14, NIV

During my many years in ministry while traveling throughout this planet I've received numerous testimonies and comments about the anointing behind my songs. I've been told by strangers and friends alike how the Spirit of God moves through my music and how their lives have been profoundly impacted as a result. I, myself, can testify to how an ordinary melody, along with some simple words, have moved my heart to tears when I least expected it. Therein lies the biggest difference between secular and sacred music. As beautiful and as grand as a melody might be, and as poetic and eloquent as some words might be molded into, without the anointing of the Holy Spirit the results are superficial and will never radically change or profoundly impact the lives of those who hear it in a positive way. Anointing is essential in the service of the Lord, and without it we are simply empty vessels needing to be filled.

I understood at a very early age that the level of anointing deposited in my life was directly connected to the trials that God had allowed me to endure. Just like the olive had to be pressed and broken for the oil to be extracted, I too needed to be shattered and torn so that the healing, restoring, and life-changing oil of anointing could flow through the wounds that at first had been the cause of so much pain. The price is great, and the road is painful and always solitary, but the reward is surely worth it. In fact, it is imperative to be broken by God for His anointing to be poured upon our lives and one day be used by Him for His glory.

New Song

I remember the months after Susi and I finalized our divorce, as I tried to find some kind of relief for my pain, I would take refuge in all things music. It wasn't anything new. It's what I always did growing up when I felt sad or lonely. Sometimes it was the hymns I sang as a child growing up in my local church. At other times it was the songs I heard on the radio or in my own personal collection. But most of all, when I sat on the piano and opened my heart before God, leaving the world and all of my problems behind, I discovered that there, in the wee hours of the morning, I would find comfort for my sorrow. Most times it was just random chords and melodies, since I had little to no interest in writing songs. But even so, the peace it brought to my heart when I began to play was unmistakable. Miraculously, as I poured myself out before God on that old, out-of-tune upright piano, I would find refuge from the storm, if only for a moment.

Even with the help of my music, it had become too painful for me to live in that old, empty house by myself. Dealing with the loneliness and bittersweet memories that would sweep over me like a hurricane around every corner of that house proved too much for me to bear, so more often than not I would wind up spending my nights at my mom's. One of those nights—out of the many sleepless ones I experienced—I sat down at the piano and began to play a melody I'd never heard before. I recall I had been questioning God that day as to why He had forgotten me and was feeling particularly distraught and overwhelmed, so I followed the notes wherever they took me. In a symbolic way, they were reflecting what my heart was feeling, and once again the tears began to flow. I can't say if it was the music or simply the way I was feeling, but that melody started to impact me in a profound way.

After a while I stopped playing, and in the silence of that moment I heard a voice tell me, "Open the Bible on top of the piano." I couldn't remember having seen it there before, but it didn't surprise me when I actually found it, as my mom had Bibles spread out all over the house. With fear and anticipation I opened it, looking for a sign or some kind of divine inspiration in my hour of need. My head was full of questions, to which I had found very few answers, and I was hoping God would speak to me and reveal His wisdom amidst my confusion.

My fingers immediately took me to Luke 15:11, and I began to read. It was the story of the prodigal son, one I had known very well and always loved reading. I identified greatly with the younger son, the one who left home, not because I was as rebellious as he was—I had always tried to be a good example, after all—but because from my childhood I longed for the unconditionally loving embrace of the father I never had, the type of hug the prodigal son received from his father upon his return home. Fatherless as I was or not, we all dream about this limitless love and about having that father who loves us in spite of our faults and rebellion. When I reached verse 20, something occurred within my spirit. It was a revelation that opened my eyes to a greater understanding of our heavenly Father's love.

*So he got up and went to his father. But while he
was still a long way off, his father saw him and was
filled with compassion for him; he ran to his son,
threw his arms around him and kissed him.*

—LUKE 15:20, NIV

A TIME OF CONFRONTATION AND BROKENNESS

In that moment I realized I was no longer alone in that room. There was a supernatural presence moving in the atmosphere that was shaking me to the core and taking over my emotions. I was afraid and fell to the floor. I felt an incomprehensible love that began to inundate my mind and my heart. I couldn't speak and felt confused and overwhelmed. Then all of sudden, as if to give me some perspective, my mind took me back to my first encounter with the Holy Spirit many years before in a youth camp I had attended. I was barely seventeen years old when I experienced something similar that forever changed my relationship with God.

I remember I had just arrived at the camp with the intention of having a good time with my church friends. If God spoke to me, fine, but in all honesty it wasn't something I was looking for. As it happens, the very first day of camp, between the late evening and early hours of that morning, when all my friends were fast asleep I began to feel something strange inside my heart. I'm not one who suffers from phobias or is easily frightened. I'm not afraid of the dark, nor the boogeyman. But this was a paralyzing fear that began to overtake me and made me want to look for help immediately, which is exactly what I did. I got up and knocked on my aunt's door. (She was my pastor at the time.) She and the youth pastor took me to the prayer room and, after seeing my emotional state, asked me what I was feeling. I could barely get a word out to answer. All I could do was cry and tell them I was afraid. I felt as if an internal struggle was going on inside of me, a battle for my soul, and I had a decision to make. Seeing my condition and hearing me speak made them realize they needed to intercede for my life immediately.

We spent what seemed like hours in that room praying and asking God to do something with my life. I've never cried as much as I did that night in camp. When the fear subsided, I felt the presence of God in a powerful and tangible way, and it was glorious! I realized in that moment that although I had given my life to God, He wanted more. I was confronted with my questionable and selfish attitude toward those around me and my lack of conviction regarding my leadership responsibilities. I had been living a double life, and God was requiring a higher standard from me. That night in camp I left my plans and my dreams in the hands of the One who had the grandest of plans for my life and the most magnificent dreams I could ever imagine. I was finally able to find peace after giving God all of me without any conditions or reserves.

That night in front of my piano, Bible in hand, there I was once again feeling that same paralyzing fear and overwhelming anxiety I had felt so many years before as I fought through the tears and grasped for air in a desperate search for truth and God's direction. I continued reading, and the more I did, the more the story impacted me. How could this father show so much grace and mercy toward a son who had betrayed and embarrassed the family name? How could he simply forget all that he had done and take him back, as if nothing had happened? But yet there he was waiting with relentless compassion and unconditional love for his son to one day come back home. Day after day, rain or shine, nothing deterred his hope as he got up each and every morning, time after time, thinking, "Maybe today will be the day my son returns."

I finally got the picture. I, once and for all, understood the lesson that was being presented to me, and it all started with a question: Who are you not to forgive? Those words broke my heart into a million pieces, leaving them scattered throughout that living room floor. I had no defense. There weren't any wounds I could show or words I could muster to justify my actions before God. It was as if a veil had been lifted from my eyes and everything had become crystal clear.

When I saw God's heart and compared it to mine, I realized I had been a hypocrite, a selfish man who had been incapable of sharing—and worse, unwilling to share—what by grace he had received. I was shown in my mind, as if a movie were playing before me, the countless times I insulted Susi, letting her know with precise detail how little I thought of her. I witnessed the many occasions she had asked me to forgive her and how all I could summon from the depths of my heart were looks of contempt and rejection. I pictured myself humiliating her, reminding her with every chance I had of all the evil she had done and showing no love nor compassion even though I knew she was alone, slowly and desperately drowning in an ocean of guilt and shame. In fact, in spite of knowing that I was the only one with a life preserver, the only one who could rescue her and grant her another chance at a normal existence, I stood on the shore alongside all her other critics and accusers, crossed my arms without mercy, and allowed her to die in that decisive and crucial moment of her life when she needed me the most.

In that moment I felt ashamed and incapable of accepting God's love. How could I have been so cruel with my words one instant and then stood in the altar to worship God the next? How profound was God's compassion with me in those days, that even when I didn't live up to what I was singing, He still showed up. Maybe He felt sorry for me, understanding what I was going through and how difficult it had been. Maybe He saw something in me that gave Him hope I would one day change my ways. Whatever the case, just like He did in that camp years before, He was once again confronting me, asking me for something more.

77

This time, however, He wasn't looking for me to give Him my talents or gifts, nor simply to trust Him with my dreams and aspirations. No, God was wanting something I hadn't been willing to give up, something with greater value. This had proved to be a lot more difficult for me to surrender than anything else in my life, though doing so would change my destiny forever. He was asking me to forgive. I had been fighting for months with the pain of Susi's betrayal, and although in front of those around me it seemed I had it all under control, deep inside I was destroyed. The anger and bitterness were slowly consuming me, and peace had made itself scarce and was nowhere to be found. Once more the deciding moment had arrived: a crossroads that would represent a before-and-after in my life.

I knew what I needed to do, and before God that night I finally surrendered. In doing so, I felt the embrace of my heavenly Father, the One I had longed for since this all began. He overtook me with His love and grace, showering me with compassion and understanding and finally whispering in my ear, "I'm here. You are not alone."

Till that moment God had remained silent, and I truly thought He had forgotten about me. "Maybe I'm not important enough to waste His time. Maybe He'll never answer," I had mused. But that night, just when I thought all was lost, in the stillness of that dark and empty room the God of my youth showed up in an extraordinary and supernatural way. I once again felt the peace that had evaded me for so long, bringing calm to my restless and desperate soul. My soul, which minutes before had been drowning in an sea of anxiety and hopelessness, had now found rest and refuge with just a few words from the Master. I understood that He had never abandoned me but was simply waiting for the perfect time to reveal His plan and purpose for my life. In the end, I understood that forgiveness was always the key to my freedom, the key that would open the doors to a life of abundant blessings, profound peace, and powerful anointing. It was all part of His plan from the beginning.

WHAT IF I FORGIVE HER

Forgive my wife? Could it be possible? Was there still a way to recover all that had been lost and somehow restore our love? After all that had transpired, could a miracle be within reach to fix this disaster that was our broken marriage?

Searching for reconciliation would bring unfavorable repercussions to my already fragile ego. "What would people say?" I thought. "How will they see me? Perhaps as someone with a weak character, since I'd be going back on everything I had said and done since Susi confessed." I recall in my ignorance and immaturity my exact words being, "If my wife is unfaithful to me, I would leave her without thinking twice!" Now I was considering taking her back! I knew the road to restoration would be one of embarrassment and shame before the eyes of others, including our friends and family. I understood that forgiving my wife would require having to share the burden of guilt and shame she had been carrying, and in doing so, I too would be put in a position of being pointed at and talked about.

But it was clear there was no other way around it. I knew from the beginning forgiving Susi wouldn't be a words-only decision. It would take serious commitment and some heavy lifting. I would have to take her place in the center of that storm of accusations and culpability, facing all the consequences that it entailed. But I was decided and resolute.

Thinking back, I understand now why God needed to break my heart into a million pieces. There was only one way I would accept the challenge before me and forgive the unforgivable: I needed a brand-new heart. My old way of thinking, egocentric and judgmental, would've never given way to grace, mercy, and forgiveness. That night, from the inside out, God began to make something new. There, rising from the ashes and debris of what was once a bitter and broken child, a heart according to Him was reborn, one in which logic and law gave way to compassion and grace, where anger and resentment were replaced by love and hope, and where the ways of a rebellious child bowed down to the obedience of a godly man. Transformed by the power and anointing of the Holy Spirit, I was ready to embrace forgiveness and fight for my marriage.

During that time I had been given an amazing treasure of a book called *The Freedom of Forgiveness* by David Augsburger. (I recommend it to anyone who is hurt and in desperate need of healing.) Augsburger states in his book:

> He who forgives pays a huge sum, the price of all the damage and hurt that has been done to him. If the state forgives a criminal, society is responsible for paying all the misdeeds caused by said criminal. If someone breaks an expensive family heirloom and the owner forgives the party at fault, he then takes responsibility for the loss and the culprit is set free... In forgiving, we put our anger before the sin of the guilty, voluntarily accepting responsibility for the damage done to us.[1]

The book goes on to explain:

> Forgiveness is not simply taking the easy road and looking the other way when someone has failed you. It is not the equivalent of a passing wink at sin, for it does not take being wronged lightly, and it won't accept the pious idea in pretending that evil, in reality, is not so evil. It is also not the same as just forgetting. Of course when you forgive, you forget. But to pretend that forgetting comes before forgiving is like taking the final exam to be allowed entrance into the course.[2]

After accepting Christ as my personal Savior, forgiving my wife was the most profoundly impactful decision I had ever made. The wounds were still there, and the lack of trust and all the doubts that came with it wouldn't go away immediately, but I knew deep in my heart that it was God's will, and that was good enough for me.

It always helped, in my moments of self-doubt, to reflect on the portrait of the Cross as the perfect example of forgiveness. Seeing Jesus carrying the burden of my sins and all of its painful consequences provided a shining reminder of all I needed to live up to. My debt became His debt, my mistakes His mistakes, and through it all He just kept on forgiving, without conditions or pretexts, all the way to the cross and into the grave. There would never be a better blueprint to help me put my life back together than the one portrayed on that old, rugged cross. Jesus had done it for me, and now it was my turn to do the same with Susi.

But was I brave enough? Would I be able to withstand the spiteful glances and scornful criticisms from those who surrounded us? Those questions constantly inundated my mind, but I wouldn't look back.

A New Song

God had visited me, and I had been challenged, confronted, and broken by His Holy Spirit. His glory had descended upon my life in a powerful and life-changing way, and I would never be the same.

When we speak about God's glory, the peace and happiness that being in His presence brings always come to mind. It's like having a little piece of heaven come down and fill the emptiness of our mundane lives in supernatural fashion. But God's glory is also like the dawn, bringing clarity and truth to what had once been a shadowy and false existence. That clarity brings to the forefront our imperfections, making us realize how far we still have to go. It shows us that we are not who we think we are and allows us to understand that being a victim does not give us a "get out of forgiveness" card. We are still called to show love, compassion, mercy, and grace, no matter how deep the wounds or devastating the loss.

81

That is precisely what occurred to me that night. His glory descended upon my life like the morning sun, shining a light on my true self and showing me that I still had a ways to go. I knew that I would never be the same. My life would shine bright but no longer with just my songs and abilities. I would let the world know with my life and forgiving example what God could do when repentance meets forgiveness.

God confronted me, not with rejection or punishment, not with shame or contempt, but with love and understanding. At once I could see my grave mistake clearly: I had confronted Susi with rejection and punishment instead of with love and understanding, as God had shown to me. By not meeting her repentance with forgiveness, I both extended and compounded Susi's and my suffering. I surrendered unto His will wholeheartedly. The past no longer mattered; I just wanted my wife back. I longed to feel her in my arms again, to let her know how much I still cared. I wanted her to understand that no matter what she had done, I was still the same man who loved her from the very first moment that we met.

That night was the beginning of our restoration process. Just like Susi, I had to embrace repentance, acknowledging my faults and allowing God to break me and make me new with a loving, forgiving, and merciful heart. My prayer that night was simple yet bold. I prayed that God would restore what had been lost but also that for every painful tear I had shed, somehow, somewhere, someday, a life would be impacted and blessed by our testimony.

I sat at the piano one more time and began writing the words and music to a song called "Quizás Hoy" (Maybe Today). I recall that with every melodic movement and poetic verse I put on paper, I could feel the hand of God guiding and directing each and every move. It was as though He was writing the song, and I was just a pen in His hands. The emotion, the description of the Father's longing, the chord progressions—it all came easily and without delay. I understood that God had been waiting for me to open my heart and to embrace forgiveness for Him to then pour down this powerful anointing over me.

God wants to glorify Himself in our failures. He longs to pour out His supernatural anointing over our lives, which turns the impossible into reality. He desires to takes us into a deeper understanding of His grace and love and a more profound knowledge of the characteristics of His heart. But none of this is possible if we don't accept the will of the Father. Even when it's the most difficult, the least popular, and the loneliest of paths, it's the one with the greatest rewards and what He demands from us.

Forgiveness That Frees and Restores

What is God's will? We find the best example of it on the cross. Jesus, being innocent of all charges and free of all sin, came to die cruelly and unjustly for our trespasses. Why? Why did the Son of God have to descend from heaven and painfully die on a cross? Couldn't He simply have said, "I forgive them," and have that be the end of it? With just one official decree from heaven, all suffering would have been avoided by the son of God, the King of kings and Lord of lords. But all sin—our sin, which sent Jesus to the cross— leaves a debt, a debt that can't be canceled with heavenly decrees or eloquent words.

Years ago someone shared this metaphor with me:

> One day someone invites you to their house for dinner. It's not just any house but the house of one of the richest families in the city. When you arrive, you pass through the grand entryway of this luxurious home to find a table set for a king. The finest silverware and most expensive china your eyes have ever seen are laid out, and a place at the table has been reserved for you and your family. As you look through the crowd you see presidents, kings, and dignitaries all partaking in friendly chatter as they wait for dinner to be served.

The owner of the house explains that all the plates, glasses, and utensils that will be used throughout the night form part of a rare vintage collection that has been passed down from generation to generation. They are all one of a kind and extremely priceless.

They begin to serve the food, and of course, the worst thing you can ever imagine happens. One of the plates slips from your fingers, crashing violently on the floor and breaking into a thousand pieces. In that moment your face says it all. You want the earth to open up and swallow you whole. Feeling like the worst person in the world and wishing you somehow had a time machine close by, you come to grips with the fact that there's no way to avoid the inevitable: someone has to take responsibility for the broken plate. The only problem is, the plate is irreplaceable, and no amount of money in the world could bring it back. The only viable option you have is throwing yourself at the mercy of the owners and begging for forgiveness. To your surprise, forgiveness is offered immediately, and you are set free from all consequences.

However, one must remember that the plate is still always going to be broken, and the collection will never be whole, as one of the most important pieces will forever be missing. A debt remains open that someone must assume. And of course there is still the pain of losing such a valuable heirloom. The owners of the house have freed you from the debt, taking upon themselves the consequences of the broken plate. But every time the table is served an empty space forever reminds them of the priceless piece that could never be replaced.

That's how sin is: always leaving a debt that, without exemption, must somehow be paid. Every mistake and misdeed that has ever been committed leaves consequences that have to be dealt with.

The forgiveness we are called by God to extend to others is rooted in His mercy. It is the radical act of accepting the consequences of sin while knowing all along you were the innocent party. It's carrying the blame, paying the debt, and never sending the invoice to those who have wronged you. Forgiveness frees the guilty of all shame and restores him to his original position.

That's what the father did with the prodigal son. When he met his son on that road to redemption, the father didn't ask him how much money he had left, nor did he judge him for wearing tattered and unclean clothes. He didn't position him beneath what he was and what he always would be: his son!

In fact, the Word of God leads us to believe that the father never held a grudge nor felt resentment toward his son but instead constantly dreamed of the day he would safely and miraculously return. The father showed forgiveness from the instant the son decided, in rebellion and pride, to leave his house until the day that he returned home with a humble and contrite heart.

To forgive also has secondary benefits that gives us an insight as to why God wants us to apply it constantly.

1. To forgive is not a sign of weakness but rather requires great courage and effort.
2. Forgiveness displays an affinity for God's heart.
3. Forgiveness frees not only the culprit but also the victim.

Anger, hostility, and contempt are harmful emotions that slowly suffocate our dreams, extinguish our hopes, and cancel God's purpose for our lives. They tie you to an instant, encasing you in a moment of your past and end up governing your present and annulling your destiny. I remember being caught up in my anger and bitterness for months, reliving my wife's sin over and over again in my head. They were scenes on an endless loop, constantly repeating themselves without mercy. Day and night, there was simply no escaping the painful memories of all that she had done. I wouldn't eat, I couldn't sleep, and finding no way out, I felt myself slowly dying inside. I never imagined that what the world saw as weakness—the option that no one dared offer me in those first days—would be the act that put God's hand in motion to free me from captivity and restore what the enemy had tried to steal. Forgiveness set me free!

WISE COUNSEL

In my heart it became clear what I needed to do, but how to do it had me worried and nervous. I still struggled with the painful emotions of Susi's betrayal and the rejection I felt because of it, and I would frequently be overtaken by thoughts of rage and resentment, which crashed over me like tsunami waves. I decided to go to the fountain of wisdom that had been a staple of my life as far back as I could remember, the woman who had acted as the greatest example I had ever seen of what it meant to live a life of integrity and faith: my mother. She had always given me wise counsel, so the next the day I decided to ask for a few minutes of her time.

Like always, she didn't hesitate and sat down with me to listen to my concerns, as she had done so many times before. Opening up my heart, I let her know how God had spoken to me the night before and that although I had decided to embrace forgiveness, I still felt doubt and anxiety about calling Susi and trying to give our marriage one more try. I asked for her advice.

I expected the reaction of a mother whose son had his heart broken, a reaction similar to mine perhaps—full and anger and spite and without compassion or mercy. But instead I was shocked to hear her say, "We've been praying for God to touch your heart. We believe He can still work a miracle in your marriage, and we want to be a part of that process." Her words were full of love and support. She never said a negative thing about Susi. There was not one comment about the past, nor of any of the terrible things that had transpired. She told me she and my grandmother had been praying for my inner healing but most of all for Susi and her fragile heart. She let me know the decision of getting divorced, in her opinion, was a rushed one and not part of God's plan.

However, more importantly, and what impacted me most profoundly, were the words of faith and affirmation that pierced my heart and broke down the barriers that were keeping me from fulfilling God's purpose for my life. She said, "There is nothing impossible for God." Those words filled me with hope and gave me the courage I needed to take the next step. It was exactly what I longed to hear but was afraid of admitting.

I don't know why or how the idea came about, but I asked my mom for her blessing in inviting Susi to our family Christmas vacation that was soon approaching. I saw in her eyes and heard in her voice the answer that gave me the peace I so desperately needed, which put everything in motion. She answered with two simple words: "Of course." We finished with a prayer, and I felt the assurance one feels only when you know you are in God's perfect will.

It's important to recognize that the peace that passes all understanding only comes to our lives when we walk in God's purpose and design. It doesn't matter if the world around us is falling apart or if support and belief are nowhere to be found. In whatever the situation, "if God is with us, who can be against us?" (Rom. 8:31, niv). He has the final word, and He says, "We know that in all things God works for the good of those who love him, who have been called according to his purpose" (Rom. 8:28, niv). If you're walking in God's purpose for your life, He will open the doors and give you the strength necessary to reach your goals and fulfill your dreams, regardless of how impossible it all might appear to be.

I had made up my mind to call Susi and to speak with restrained emotions, without hurtful words, and with a little bit of hope. But I was still beyond nervous to have a real conversation again the woman who not so long ago had stolen my heart, who only a little while ago had made me laugh, dream, and of course, cry.

But how would she react? We hadn't spoken for a few weeks, and I was unaware of her emotional state. I had treated her so badly with every effort she made to get close to me, and for sure she would have her defenses up the moment she heard my voice. Again, the nerves got the best of me, but regardless, I picked up the phone and dialed her number. As I heard her voice on the other side of the line, I felt something I thought I would never feel again. The sound of her voice took me back to the first time we talked on the phone years before. A nervous, butterflies-in-your-stomach feeling fell over me, and I was surprised. I noticed she sounded different, more sure of herself but with the same butterflies as me. I asked her about her mom and dad, all the while going over in my head how I was going to invite her to our trip. She told me everyone was well and that she was also feeling better. It felt strange to hear her speak in such a disconnected and distant way, but such are the residuals of divorce. The intimacy gets lost, along with the habits that once made you feel so comfortable.

But, how I missed her friendship!

After a few minutes on the line I mentioned my grand idea, inviting her to our family vacation in January. I couldn't see her face, but I sensed her shaky voice on the other side of the phone, letting me know how surprised she was with my proposal. She asked if I had mentioned the idea to my mom. I said yes and that everything was approved by the family. Her response was quick and what I hoped to hear: she would be coming with us on vacation. We hung up with a courteous good-bye, one that made us both feel uncomfortable and weird. But in reality we couldn't ask for anything more after all we had been through. Her actions and my words had created an undesirable and disastrous situation. It was crazy to see two hearts who had once been so full of love now struggling with a simple good-bye.

A GLIMPSE OF HAPPINESS

I watched her arrive with her mom, and as she parked I approached the car and helped her with the door. After a polite kiss on the cheek and a friendly, "How've you been?" we walked to the banks of a canal that ran beside my mom's house. There, staring at her face as we were together alone for the first time in a long time, I couldn't contain myself. I reached out and caressed her cheek. I couldn't even talk, but with a knot in my throat I whispered three simple words: "I've missed you." She reciprocated, "Me too."

There was silence as we profoundly embraced, and for an instant, for just a moment in time, everything was OK. The past didn't exist, and our world was perfect. It was as if God was giving us a glimpse of the happiness that could be ours, if we only we gave forgiveness a chance.

We walked back together just as everyone was gathering for the trip. We had a long and difficult road ahead, and although doubt was still present in our hearts and we would proceed with caution, hope was in the air.

Chapter 6

RETURN TO ME

by Susana Rodríguez

ICONTINUED MY MORNING ROUTINE of praying at the park, my father always supportive and vigilant, right by my side. Both my parents knew how fragile I still was and would watch over me day and night, providing loving words and spiritual guidance through my most difficult moments. But I, struggling with the drastic change in my life, still wouldn't eat and had a hard time sleeping. I was disconnected from the world and didn't watch TV, nor had any other form of outside information. All I would do is read the Bible. The sun and moon would come and go, and I continued hiding in my solitary bubble, not wanting to deal with anything or anyone.

I began to realize one day that my parents' house was going to be my permanent home for an undetermined amount of time; therefore, I needed to help them out financially. I started looking for a job and found one at a local veterinary clinic. The day of the interview I found it difficult to even dress myself, let alone leave the house. I arrived at the veterinarian's office with a face full of tears but composed myself and gathered enough strength, with my mom's help, to walk reluctantly into the building. They handed me a formal application to complete before the interview, and I continued to swallow my tears as I filled out the paperwork for a job I needed but definitely didn't want. All I thought about was Ricardo and how at one time we had a home and shared a life and so many dreams together. But those thoughts always ended up with the same conclusion: I'm where I deserve to be. I sinned, and therefore, I lost.

I remember one of the questions I had to answer on the application being a multiple choice question about my marital status. I was to mark *M* for married, *D* for divorced, or *W* for widowed. I stared at that question for several minutes trying to figure out how to answer. I still found it so hard to believe that I was no longer married to Ricardo. I had become another statistic, a *D* for divorced. I wanted a moment to explain myself to the office manager, and as weird as it sounds, a chance to say, "I'm sorry for the indiscretion, but that is not who I truly am."

In the end, they gave me the job. I don't even know why. I think they felt sorry for me. They told me I was overqualified to work there, but if I wanted it, the job was mine. I wanted nothing to do with the public, so I asked to be assigned to the back with the animals. I didn't want to deal with answering any questions from friends, family, or any other curious person who might show up at the clinic.

On my first day of work my mom dropped me off early. As she was driving off I wanted to run after her, like a little girl on her first day of school. In truth, I felt like a child, afraid and lonely, overwhelmed by my pain. The vet, seeing my emotional state, asked me why I was so sad. I didn't know what to tell him. Everything was so fresh in my mind. The wound hadn't healed, and my broken heart was in no condition to assume the daily routines of a normal life. I couldn't take it, and apologizing, I excused myself and started walking home.

During that walk I began to go over everything that had occurred: my confession to Ricardo, the divorce, and the relentless pain that had become such a common part of my life. I started to cry and talk to God. "How long will I have to suffer?" I asked. "Will I forever be the person people want nothing to do with? How can I ever overcome this terrible chapter in my life?" I really felt

I was doing all I could with my prayer life and nourishing myself with the Word of God, which was like daily manna from heaven to my spirit. But I still felt lost and hopeless. It was a long walk, and feeling as if I wouldn't make it, I stopped at a pay phone to call my mother. I also didn't need anyone seeing me walk alone through the streets of Miami, thereby giving them more ammunition to point fingers and judge me. Sitting there waiting for my mom in a bus bench, I started going over in my head the amount of suffering and pain I had gone through and once again questioned God as to when the burden would be lifted.

HOW MUCH LONGER, GOD?

My mom picked me up, and when we arrived at her house I went straight to my room to pray. This was my comfort, my strength. But those questions I would ask God were constantly in my mind. How long would I be punished for what I'd done? Although I had grown up in church, I still didn't fully understand God's love and forgiveness. I felt blind and confused. Weeping before God, I kept pleading, "I'm begging You, please, please, forgive me!"

That night my mother invited me to a small prayer service that was being held in a nearby city. She explained that a friend of hers had recommended coming to the prayer service since God had been using an evangelist who was visiting from out of town in a powerful way. I accepted her invitation, and we left together. During that time I hungered for all things God, but I still felt a heavy burden over my life, one that constantly kept weighing down my heart. When we arrived, I noticed it was being held in an old house in the menacing side of town I always tried to avoid, and I hesitated going in. My mother finally convinced me to get out of the car when she saw a friend of hers entering the home. It was an old school prayer service, and I felt out of place. I was skeptical of everything and everyone, but putting my doubts aside, I opened my heart to God that night.

They sang a couple of songs from the hymn book, and while the piano was softly playing in the background I whispered one more time to God, "Father, I'm begging You. Please forgive me. Please forgive me!" Suddenly, I felt the gentle touch of someone's hand over my head, and as I opened my eyes I saw him standing over me. It was the guest evangelist who had been leading the service. He proceeded to lean over me, speaking the words that I so longed to hear and that would finally bring end to the captivity of shame and guilt that had been keeping my heart and soul in bondage: "You have been forgiven and are set free from your past. Why can't you accept God's forgiveness for your life?" I finally understood all I had read in the Bible but had been foolishly reluctant to apply in my life. It was God's forgiveness! God's grace! God's love for me! In between tears all I could say was, "Thank you. Thank you!"

The key to overcoming the paralyzing effects of sin and the world of guilt and self-pity that accompany it is to walk into God's forgiveness, embracing His unconditional love and unparalleled mercy as a reality in your life.

A weight had been lifted from my shoulders. The Spirit of God was palpable in that old house, and I was afraid of even opening up my eyes. I didn't want that sweet, peaceful, life-altering moment of being in God's presence to end, and it didn't. It followed me home. I spent that whole night awake, worshiping and thanking God for His love and grace and for giving me the gift of freedom. My heart was overcome with joy. I remember sitting on the edge of my bed and placing my hand on the covers, imagining Jesus holding it. He was my Friend, my Savior, and He had remembered me. Although I was till divorced, displaced, and without employment, I wasn't alone.

This revelation of God's forgiveness transformed my understanding of the Scriptures. I always loved reading the Psalms, but after I finally came to understand the profound, unconditional, and total forgiveness of God, I began to read them again in a whole new light. When we read Psalm 51, we get a glimpse of David's broken and contrite heart, searching and desperately needing forgiveness and mercy. We perceive in his words a sincere, repentant man with profound remorse for his actions.

My sacrifice, O God, is a broken spirit; a broken
and contrite heart you, God, will not despise.

—PSALM 51:17, NIV

This type of spirit moves the hand of God to save, heal, and restore. David was freed from the guilt of his transgression not by his sacrifice but because of his contrite heart. He humbled himself before God, knowing he was unworthy of His mercy and grace. He couldn't change the past. The damage was final, and nothing he could do would make it any different. The verdict had been announced, and he had been found guilty on all charges. There was a price to pay, but in surrendering to the mercy of an all-powerful and merciful God, he had found forgiveness where a death sentence should've been. Instead of encountering rejection and punishment, he found acceptance and a loving embrace from the God of second chances. God Himself said David was a man according to His own heart. I finally realized that if David could be redeemed from his transgressions, there was hope for me to be restored as well. For the first time in a long while I began to believe that God saw value in me.

SECURE IN GOD'S FORGIVENESS

Since that prayer meeting and the revelation I gained, my prayers had been fortified and my words filled with authority. I was no longer that scared little girl full of doubt and guilt but a confident, godly woman who understood she had been forgiven and would no longer allow herself or anyone to remind her of her past. For the first time, instead of groveling under the bed, I thoroughly enjoyed my intimate conversations with God, and during them I began to ask with fervor for the healing of Ricardo's wounds. I prayed he would soften his hardened heart, the one that was full of anger and hate and had eventually turned to stone from all the pain I had caused. I continued my weekly visits to his house at night when he was asleep, declaring that one day God would restore what the enemy had stolen from our lives and I would be able to return to my husband and my home.

I garnered the courage to write a letter explaining my metamorphosis to Ricardo, letting him know how much I still loved him and what God was doing in my life. Among other things, I mentioned a song that arrived straight from heaven into my life during that time. It was called "He's Been Faithful" by Damaris Carbaugh and the Brooklyn Tabernacle Choir. Oh, what a blessing it had been for my parents and I! God's faithfulness had been so obvious every step of the way, and that song was an anthem of gratitude straight from our hearts to God's. As I listened to it I would thank Him for all I had, although it might not have seemed like much. I was forever grateful for the tears and the joys, for the process, and the hope of an amazing result in the end.

After leaving the letter at Ricardo's door, I didn't hear from him at all, although in truth, I wasn't expecting much of a response. In the end, my only purpose was to tell the man I had been married to that I still loved and missed him dearly. It wasn't another apology letter begging for forgiveness but instead a sincere and heartfelt explanation that my reality and my purpose had changed. In it I also laid out plans to visit our church that coming Sunday after not going for a few months.

Sunday couldn't arrive soon enough. I remember being so emotional and nervous when it did. I was astonished at the fact that I had found the courage to walk into that church one more time, and I was over the moon that I would be able to hear Ricardo lead worship. I missed that so much! What had once felt like an unwanted burden as I was constantly being dragged to church for one rehearsal, meeting, or service after the other, had now become the desire of my heart. I always knew God had anointed Ricardo to be used in a powerful way through worship, and from the moment we walked into the church that morning the presence of the Holy Spirit could be felt. We sat in the mezzanine, where I hoped not to draw too much attention, and as soon as we found our seats, I began to cry. Just being there emotionally overwhelmed me. I longed for my friends to come by and say hello, and it was so painful to see them all stay in their seats and pretend I wasn't even there.

When the time of worship was over, they began to pick up the offering and make the weekly announcements. I thought Ricardo was done singing, but then all of a sudden he walked back up to the altar and said, "I have a special song I'd like to sing this morning that has been a blessing to my life. It's titled 'He's Been Faithful,' and I pray it's a blessing to your life today, no matter what you might be going through."

I couldn't believe what I was hearing! Ricardo was going to sing the song I had mentioned to him earlier that week in the letter. He had searched for it, purchased the accompaniment track, rehearsed it, and was now going to share it with the congregation! Was this a gift for me? Was he trying to tell me something? Tears just poured down my face, and I felt compelled to lift my hands and worship God with all my heart. His faithfulness went far beyond anything I could comprehend. It was more than I deserved, leaving my heart indebted and grateful. I couldn't contain my joy.

During that service our eyes crossed paths from a distance and then slowly lost each other again. There was so much I wanted to tell him, so much I wanted to share with my old friend. I longed to let him know about all the Bible stories I had discovered through the teachings of my father and the long walks I'd been taking in the park with Jesus by my side. But all those stories would have to wait. Ricardo's heart was nowhere near hearing what God had been doing in my life, or so I thought.

Weeks went by without a word from Ricardo, yet I continued interceding for his heart and the healing he so desperately needed. Now there were four of us praying with fervor and faith: my mother; my father; his cousin, Rachel, who never stopped talking to Ricardo about forgiveness and what God was doing in my life; and of course, myself. Rachel is small in stature, but what she lacked in height she more than made up for in heart and passion. She had been caring, selfless, and resolute in fighting for the restoration of our marriage, and I will forever be grateful to her for that. She didn't concern herself with Ricardo's anger, nor his defiance toward God's will, but instead continued to confront him with God's healing power, the power to breathe life into that which had been dead. Meanwhile, I continued to trust in God. He had been silent, but that only assured me that He was working on something special.

Let's Talk

One night as I was deep in prayer the phone rang. I quickly heard a knock on my bedroom door and my mother's voice call out, "Ricardo is on the phone. He wants to talk to you!" I could hear my father get out of bed and run to my room. He poked his head in through the half-open door and asked, "What's going on?" So much time had passed without a mere word or call from him, but for better or worse, we were ready.

I answered the phone, "Hello!"

"How are you?" he asked.

I responded amicably but briefly.

"Can you come by the bookstore? I'd like to talk to you alone," he said.

My heart was beating out of my chest. He wanted to see me in private. Would he insult me again? Maybe scream at me like he did in the very beginning of this horrible nightmare? I paused and remembered my conversations with God. I had promised to trust in Him no matter what, so I took a deep breath and answered, "Yes, I'll be there in a few minutes."

I spoke to my parents, letting them know I would be taking the car to meet Ricardo at the bookstore and asking them to please intercede. I got dressed, all the while asking the Holy Spirit to go before me. I knew I couldn't make it on my own.

It was already midnight when I arrived at the bookstore, and Ricardo was waiting inside. As he saw me get out of the car he unlocked the door to the shop so I could come in. He cordially greeted me and asked me to please come in and sit down. I hadn't been back to the store in quite a while, and it was painful just being there. Deep inside though, I knew God was with me. We sat on the floor and talked for a bit about the bookstore and all the work that went into running it. He was doing it on his own now and understood a lot better the pressure and stress associated with being there day after day.

After the initial hello and pleasantries about the shop, he went straight to the difficult and more heart-wrenching questions. Why did I destroy our marriage? What made me distance myself from our home? Although I tried to answer with full transparency, completely opening my heart for him to see, his face couldn't hide the dissolution and frustration my answers were leaving him with. In truth, there wasn't a good enough explanation for what I'd done, and there would never be one. I believe, in that moment, he finally figured it out. It was heartbreaking seeing him struggle to find a rational explanation for the irrational and chaotic.

On the other hand, I wondered, Why now? Why talk about the past now, and not the day I got on my knees and confessed my indiscretions? Why was it that months had to pass and our divorce had to be finalized before he could bring himself to hear what I had to say? If only we could've given each other time and been patient before running to get divorced! But there we were, sitting in the dark on the floor of our bookstore, wondering what went wrong and if somehow we could find a way to fix it. I glanced at his face through my tears and saw him wiping his own. I begged

God to comfort his heart and bring him some well-deserved rest to his tormented mind.

After a few minutes of awkward silence he asked me how my spiritual life was and if I felt any different about myself after all that had happened. I was anxious to let him know about my newfound relationship with Jesus, my Friend and constant companion, and what I was learning from the Scriptures. It's incredible how we can hear the same stories over and over again without knowing how to apply them to our lives. It's only when conflict arises and a new perspective is presented that we fully understand, appreciate, and learn how to value the lessons behind them.

When I started sharing with him all the biblical stories my father had been introducing me to and he saw how profoundly engaged I was, his face began to change. No longer was he somber and serious but instead showed glimpses of happiness, and I was sure I even saw a smile. Ricardo could clearly see I had opened my heart and been transformed by the Word of God. I wasn't the same woman he had known. My repentant heart and contrite demeanor had allowed me to capture his attention once more. My words were confident and full of affirmation, and there was evidence of Jesus in me. After all, I had been made new.

> It is for freedom that Christ has set us free. Stand firm, then, and do not let yourselves be burdened again by a yoke of slavery.
>
> —GALATIANS 5:1, NIV

He asked about my family and what they thought of him after his harsh response toward me and them, especially my father. My father had made various efforts to reach him, but Ricardo never allowed anyone close and always treated my dad with contempt. Now, deep inside, he wanted to know if my parents still loved him. I explained that my mom and dad never held any grudges nor ill feelings toward Ricardo, understanding full well the level of pain and anger he was dealing with. The love and admiration they felt toward him never wavered and still today are deeply embedded in their hearts.

The night carried on longer than we had originally planned. It even turned into a musical gift for me as he played the songs that had been such a blessing to his life through the worst moments of this ordeal. We always had a musical connection from the very first day we spoke on the phone, and I loved it. Our musical tastes ran the full spectrum of genres and styles, and that night became a symphony of hope and inspiration, of reminiscing and new discovery. Through it all, he still sheltered his emotions, never allowing me to get too close. I understood and maintained my distance but in my mind constantly declared what God had revealed to me in Jeremiah 15:19.

STAYING THE COURSE

A month had passed since that conversation in the bookstore with Ricardo, and it was terribly difficult to deal with the silence coming from his end. I always longed to know how he was doing, both emotionally and physically. He had lost a lot of weight, and I was seriously concerned for his well-being. I took a risk and called his cousin Rachel, who also lived in his mother's house during that time. Thank God she answered the phone. She let me know his mother and grandmother had asked about me and were concerned about the way everything escalated and ultimately ended. She assured me they didn't harbor any anger or disdain toward me and only wanted peace and happiness for myself and Ricardo. They were praying for me from a distance, but out of respect for Ricardo couldn't reach out to call. All in all, it was a very uncomfortable time for everyone involved.

I asked about Ricardo and told her in detail about our conversation at the bookstore, but she already knew, since he had also opened up to her. Then she said the words I was sure I'd never hear again from anyone: "Susi, he still loves you! Stay the course, and don't stop praying. God is doing something miraculous, and we can all see it. In fact, you must be doing something right, because he's definitely different. There's a change in his attitude toward you, and we're all hopeful a breakthrough is close by." All those nights declaring and proclaiming the restoration of our marriage on earth as in it is in heaven, the many mornings I had awakened to drive myself and my mom to a prayer meeting where people had gathered in search of God's presence—all of it was finally paying off! Ricardo's and my heart were being melted and reborn by the power of prayer, and it was glorious to behold! It was clear that God was listening.

> *The eyes of the Lord are on the righteous, and His ears are attentive to their cry.*
>
> —PSALM 34:15, NIV

During that time Ricardo had taken an indefinite leave of absence from the church he had grown to love and that had been a part of his life for so many years. He was now running the bookstore full-time by himself and dealing with the Christmas rush, which was always the busiest time of the year. Rachel had let me know he had been extremely busy at work, but I was desperate to see him. I missed my husband and friend. I had gotten used to being alone, with the exception of my mom and dad, but oh, how I missed Ricardo.

That Christmas in particular was a very sad and lonely one for me. Seeing those around me getting into the Christmas spirit, busy with shopping and preparing family dinners, only added to my misery and my desire to see it pass as quickly as possible. That's not how it always had been though. In the past, Christmas was always the happiest time of the year for Ricardo and me. We had our own traditions that we loved to partake in and would always try to buy each other special gifts we thought would be appreciated. Without a doubt, it had always been a special time in which we would reflect on all things, good and bad, that had transpired during the past year. Therefore, as you can imagine, my mind was overflowing with thoughts of Christmases past and what could've been. I longed to cook special holiday meals for Ricardo once more in the comfort of our home together. I would sometimes let my mind wander and would go over in my head all the dishes I would prepare for him if we were still married. I even dared to dream about us one day having children and what it would be like to celebrate the holidays with them. I recall going over baby names and thinking about what they would look like. He wanted two, and I just one.

When Christmas Eve arrived, with its lonely, melancholy vibe, I knew I had no other choice but to hold on to Jesus and everything I had learned and experienced till that point just to make it through. I refused to let myself be dragged down by self-pity, and I did what I could, with little to no resources and zero friends around me, to make the night special. I prayed and worshiped my God. There was never a moment of disillusion in His presence, and as always, I came out the other side renewed and encouraged. I was grateful. Regardless of how little I had in my parents' house, there was love, health, and faith, all of it coming from above.

Laying in my bed in the quiet of my room, I wished Ricardo a merry Christmas, wherever he was, and told him I loved him, like I'd done every day from the moment we separated.

When Christmas day arrived, to my surprise I received a call from Ricardo. I tried to act composed, but I'm sure he noticed the emotion and nervousness behind my voice. I had such a deep desire to hear from him that when he asked how things had been I began to cry. What else could I say but the truth? "I've missed you so much," I told him, my voice shaking. There was a long silence on the other end of the line. Finally, I heard his trembling voice utter, "What would you say if I asked you to join us for our family vacation in January to Walt Disney World?"

Tears where running down my face at that point, and I couldn't bring myself to speak from the knot in my throat. My thoughts were running wild. "Am I imagining what I just heard? Could it be real?" When I didn't answer, he asked again, at which point I closed my eyes and thanked God for His faithfulness. Somehow, finding the courage, I answered, "Of course I would." I hadn't been with his family since everything had exploded and was weighed down with doubts and questions as to how they would treat me. He perceived my apprehension immediately and calmed my fears. They were all happy I would be joining them.

FULL CIRCLE

The day had arrived, and my parents were very excited. They dropped me off at his mom's, and after meeting me at the car Ricardo and I walked to a canal adjacent to the house.

I didn't know what to expect, but when we arrived at the edge of the water he took my face in his hands and gently caressed it. Like a blind man studying the factions of a face, he was memorizing every curve and detail, every perfect imperfection, and the tears began to flow, this time from both of our eyes. He glanced at me and said, "I've missed you so much, Susi." Words don't exist that can truly describe our embrace and the emotions we felt in that moment. The desire of our hearts was apparent; we knew we wanted to be together.

Regardless of what people would say, putting aside the fact that divorce papers where signed and submitted, what God had joined no man could tear apart. After having lost it all and having gone through the worst season of life anyone can possibly imagine, we had come full circle, and I was standing once more in front of the man I loved and who I knew loved me more than anything.

In that moment I couldn't help but reflect on the power of prayer. In each of the times I stood in front of his house declaring healing over a heart that was hurt and full of anger and bitterness, this is what I pictured: him with a brand-new heart, healed, and full of love and forgiveness, and myself, joyous and thankful for another opportunity. There is nothing impossible for our God. No matter how far you've gone or how dark the night might appear, if there's a heart that is willing to align itself to God's plan, there will always be a way out.

Ricardo's family had been nervous at first, and his mom took me aside to talk for a while about all that had occurred. I expected an angry, Cuban mother-in-law, but more than anything what I got was a godly woman speaking words of life and comfort to my heart. She took her time to listen to me and shared some timeless and profound words of wisdom. His grandmother was more reserved but very cordial nonetheless. I knew I still had to earn her trust by showing her I would never hurt her grandson again.

Our time in the Magic Kindgom was very, well, magical. Ricardo took me by the hand as we walked around, and we felt like two kids in a world of possibilities. Everything was beautiful in the happiest place on Earth. Even the long lines to ride the attractions seemed advantageous and were much appreciated by two hearts who had desperately longed to be together. Once again, I knew I was seeing firsthand the power of prayer in action. God was granting me the desires of my heart, and of course, unable to contain my emotions, I started to cry in one of the rides. It was a surreal moment for both of us that after suffering so much and having lost more than most could imagine, there we were, protagonists in a fairytale ending.

I'd like to tell you that everything returned to normal after the trip, but I'd be lying. Ricardo had days in which he would be overcome with emotional waves of anger and confusion that would rapidly intensify and, without warning, batter him with memories of all I had done. On several instances, in a moment of rage he would even ask me to leave. In those moments there was nothing I could do to ease his pain. I had to be patient and give him time to heal. The hand of God was over both our lives, but there were things that only he and God could work out. I understood it was a process that required resilience and trusting in God's plan.

I continued to live with my parents, and a lot of times they would see me arrive discouraged and with sadness in my heart but never defeated. We knew we had to continue interceding, however long necessary.

During one of my morning prayer times, God had told me never to allow Ricardo or anyone to insult me or remind me of what I'd done. As a child of God, I was required to act as such, accepting His love and forgiveness for my life and my transgressions and declaring myself free from the past. This word of direction from Father God both uplifted my soul and gave me an anchor that held me through the storms ahead.

Dating Again

Time went by, and Ricardo and I began to draw closer and began dating again, thought it was as if for the first time. One day he invited me to the bookstore to spend some time with him while he worked. I was scared but accepted the invitation. I wanted nothing to do with the public for fear they would question where I'd been and what had happened. Many people had already found out and were upset at my hurting Ricardo the way I did. Every sin committed under heaven has its consequences, and I had to confront mine, one way or the other. I couldn't run away from it and knew I had to keep my head held high, as someone who had found grace and forgiveness in Jesus Christ would. I asked God for thicker skin and a fortified heart for what I was sure awaited me as soon as the doors opened.

Ricardo continued to invite me to the bookstore and sometimes would even entrust me to oversee it in his absence. His faith in me was returning slowly but surely. Like a bridge being rebuilt, little by little he was letting me closer to his heart. I tried my best to impress him and worked hard to win him over in the time he allotted me by his side. I would organize the music and books and kept everything tidy and clean. I would also read as much as possible in the slow part of the day or whenever I had a chance.

One day, after overhearing someone make a derogatory comment about me, those feelings of sadness and shame began to overtake me once more. I questioned whether or not I would ever be able to regain the dignified and beloved reputation I once enjoyed as Ricardo's wife. How much time would have to pass before they would see a different Susi, other than just a sinner? Feeling broken and displaced, I asked God what I'd never asked before: Why had this happened to me? After all, wasn't I born in church and raised in a Christian home? Didn't I maintain my integrity as a godly woman till the day I was married? How could He ever use me if I was broken in the eyes of the world? No one came into the bookstore during those few minutes, which seemed like hours, and as I had become accustomed to, I began to clean, composing myself and wiping the tears from my eyes during the process. I knew full well I couldn't allow myself to go into that dark and lonely place of self-pity and shame, where hopes and dreams went to die, so I began to worship. I learned during this experience that whatever I had or lacked, and whether I was loved or forsaken, forgiven or judged, my worship should never be influenced by anything else other than my heartfelt gratitude and God's undeniable sovereignty.

As I was worshiping, the UPS man came in with an order of books Ricardo had placed for a customer. Opening the box and going over the merchandise, I noticed there was one extra book, which I assumed had been sent by mistake. I put it aside to return it the next day when something told me to open it. The book was *Postcards From Heaven* by Claire Cloninger. It aroused my curiosity, so I picked it up and began to read it from back to front, something I'd always done since I was a child. The first phrase I read immediately caught my attention: "Dear child of mine." With just those words I began to cry, and my heart nervously started to accelerate. I sat down to avoid falling and continued reading.

Dear child of mine,

I am the God of all comfort. I will hold you in arms of compassion and sing you My healing song of grace. I will touch the wounds within you, and in my perfect season, I will lift you from this place of pain. But I want you to know that as I am healing you, I am also creating within you a healing ministry of your own. For to be healed by Me is to be made a healer. You see, the very comfort that I am working into your broken heart through the power of My words and the love of My people is meant to be recycled. Some day when your heart has grown strong again, I will send someone into your life who is as broken as you are today. And the compassion I am pouring into you now will flow from you into that hurting soul. You will resonate with his pain. You will reach into the depth of your own healing and love him back to life for me. What a precious vessel you will be to me then. A vessel once humbled and hurt and then healed to be a healer.

This is my plan for you,

God[1]

I was on my knees, overwhelmed with emotions, by the time I finished reading. I knew then that God would one day turn the ugliness of what had been my vile and sinful life into a precious vessel for His service and glory for all the world to see.

Chapter 7

SMELLS LIKE RAIN

by Ricardo Rodríguez

THAT VACATION BECAME one of the most memorable for Susi, myself, and my family. Even my grandmother, who didn't enjoy going out of the house much, had decided to join us, making it all that much more special. For Susi and myself, it was without a doubt historic, establishing a before-and-after in our relationship. We had put aside our pain and our past and simply saw ourselves as two people getting to know each other again. After not being together for so long, we even held hands, and it was magical. We shared a soda and rode our favorite rides together, feeling once more like a young couple in love.

I can imagine my family must have had their nerves on edge waiting for something to explode at any moment, but it never happened. Being surrounded by those who truly loved us and only wanted the best for our lives filled us with much-needed confidence and an inexplicable peace. Understandably, it was much more difficult for Susi at first, not knowing what my family's reaction would be, but they all treated her with love and affection, never mentioning anything about the past. It was as if nothing had ever happened. That trip was an oasis in the middle of the arid desert we had both been traveling through and helped prepare us for the long and difficult journey that awaited us when we returned home.

A New Beginning

There were many ups and downs in the months that followed, as you can imagine, and not everything returned to normal as quickly as we both would've liked. Forgiveness was just the first step in the long road to restoring our marriage, but we were focused and determined, staying on track within God's perfect plan. We couldn't ask for more.

I will tell you there were days I didn't even want to see Susi, not to mention speak to her. Everything that had transpired was still fresh in my mind, and the memories would harass my very soul with frequent and unexpected waves of rage and bitterness. I recall so many times waking up in the middle of the night drenched in a cold sweat after having one of the many nightmares I suffered through. I knew it was all part of the process and there was no way around it, but it was still incredibly hard.

On the other hand, Susi demonstrated great patience and resilience. Those were very turbulent days for both of us, but they were especially hard for her, and even though she could've easily said, "Enough," she always displayed a humble and passive spirit that quickly helped to diffuse whatever volatile situation she might've been facing. In fact, every time I would go into one of my fits of rage, she would immediately get on her knees in prayer, asking God for the healing of my wounded heart and peace for my tormented soul.

Little by little I started noticing a change in my perspective. It was becoming harder and harder to see her just through the eyes of disdain and anger, even in those moments when I had no self-control and would get overwhelmed with horrible memories. I began to notice that whenever I would bring to light her sinful past, mercilessly pointing out in disgust all of her transgressions, something would happen inside of me that would quickly put a halt to my judgmental and condemning nature. God would place Himself in front of her, reminding me of His love and mercy. This shouldn't have surprised me. After all, He is our advocate and our shield of protection. When the accusers come knocking at our door to judge and condemn, God stands in front, like a mighty giant, defending us. This is what He did for Susi, and the effect it had on me was transformative. I began to see everything through a filter, one that would hide all of her sins and shortcomings, revealing only a pure and clean heart transformed by God's grace and forgiveness. When God stood in front of my wife, the fight was over; my battle was in vain.

I came to understand that the secret to overcoming the strategy of the ever-accusing enemy and defeating him once and for all is not found in the sharpness of the sword, nor the length of the lance. It will never be in the eloquence of our words, nor our profound knowledge of the Law. The key to being victorious in the face of whatever giants this life will have us confront is found in our total submission to the will of an almighty and merciful God. Letting Him fight for us is the only way to guarantee victory, especially in the face of insurmountable odds.

The more I would lift my sword to attack, the more Susi humbled herself and let God go before her. When my words were released like arrows with the purpose of offending and wounding, she would ease my ire and disarm my anger by showing temperance and understanding. It was a genius and divine strategy that, with time, made my anger dissipate and my appreciation for her grow even more with every passing day.

> *A gentle answer turns away wrath, but a harsh word stirs up anger.*
>
> —PROVERBS 15:1, NIV

One of the most trying obstacles that couples who have encountered infidelity in their marriage have to negotiate is the reestablishing of trust. It's an incredible challenge that requires patience and time to overcome. It can't be faked, nor put aside, but rather must be dealt with head-on, with sincere effort and a resolute mind-set. My trust in Susi had been shattered and wound up being one of the hardest things to regain on our way to restoration. But she did her part.

When trust is lost in a marriage, regaining it requires much patience and the willingness to change established routines that had once been acceptable and taken for granted. If lies are uncovered, betrayals are committed, and transparency has been lost in a relationship, what more can we expect from the victim than to lack trust and to question everything and everyone? Susi understood this from the very beginning, and it never had to be explained. One thing she did in particular helped tremendously and eased my doubts and suspicions. No matter where she went, whether a McDonald's around the corner or the mall across town, she was always accompanied by her mother or her father. She didn't leave any opening for the enemy to sow seeds of suspicion in those who had cruelly judged her, nor in my still fragile heart.

And that's how it all started, with slow but steady steps, trusting in God and His promises for our marriage. We dated for a while, Susi still living with her parents and I living between my house and my mom's. We went out often, continuing the process of getting to know each other again, always with caution for both our sakes.

Unexpected Changes

Everything we experienced during those turbulent and painful months happened before the beginning of what today we consider our ministry, the one God so graciously placed in our hands more than fifteen years ago. We weren't public figures then, and our circle of friends was small to say the least. It was also a much different world than today's. *Social media* was a phrase no one had even heard of yet, and living off the grid simply meant not having an answering machine. So the importance of the church in our lives and relationship at that time can't be overstated.

Back then, the church we attended was the center of our lives, and we served there faithfully for many years. It was my comfort zone, where I felt appreciated by the congregation and found joy fulfilling God's purpose every Sunday morning as I lead worship. It surely never crossed my mind to walk away from it all, including my friends and everyone I had come to know as family since I was an adolescent. In all honesty, my fear of a world in which that church wasn't the center of my life limited the reach of my dreams to the ceiling of that building. But God's plans were different, and even though I didn't see it at the moment, they were better.

Up until then, the will of God for my life had been to serve in church, and for me it was more than enough. It brought me happiness, and I did it with great satisfaction for as long as I could remember. I never longed to travel, nor to record for the sake of being famous. I didn't dream of standing on a grand stage and having multitudes applaud and exalt my talent. My mind couldn't imagine a scenario in which I would win awards for projects I'd done or songs I'd written. It sounds strange, I know, but I always lived my life focused on the task at hand, and nothing else really mattered. I'm not saying it's wrong to dream, nor that it's foolish to establish worthwhile goals, working hard to reach them; however, we shouldn't live our lives discarding the godly present we've been blessed with for a future that might never reveal itself. Every day is a gift from above, and we should appreciate it as such.

In the years I've been in music ministry, I've had the amazing privilege of meeting many young and talented kids who were filled with a similar, sincere desire to serve God. I've seen their eyes full of passion, commitment, and humility—the kind undeniably required when you answer the ultimate call to arms in the army of the Lord. I've seen them serve in small and seemingly insignificant venues, the ones without much fanfare nor earthly reward, and they did it with devotion, excellence, and joy. They've been examples to follow and inspiring in their own right.

On the other hand, I've also had the undesirable experience of staring into eyes that were filled with illusions of grandeur and indispensability, eyes that were focused from the very beginning on reaching the pinnacle of earthly success through social popularity and, in doing so, remaining sadly out of touch with God's purpose for their lives. I've witnessed them strive for awards and recognition, working tirelessly to achieve their goals through self-promotion and ego-driven dedication. Every facet of their plan for success was organized to the last detail with one purpose in mind: to be the best and reach the top, assuming once they got there satisfaction and reward would soon follow. But that couldn't be further from the truth, and the Bible couldn't be any clearer on the topic. It says:

> For those who exalt themselves will be humbled,
> and those who humble themselves will be exalted.
>
> —MATTHEW 23:12, NIV

> His master replied, "Well done, good and faithful
> servant! You have been faithful with a few things;
> I will put you in charge of many things. Come and
> share your master's happiness!"
>
> —MATTHEW 25:23, NIV

Those of us who have been called to serve must remember the servant always looks to do the will of the Master, wherever and whatever that might be. He is the one who promotes, opens doors, and ultimately gives us the greatest of all rewards. It is a privilege to serve, and that service must be done with integrity, graciousness, and humility, never being taken for granted or looked upon as a burden.

I recall that during the very beginning of my relationship with Susi my joy was a life full of daily routines and void of complications. I was content leading worship at my local church and hiding behind the piano. Honestly, if it wouldn't have been for all that happened in my marriage I'd probably still be there. I reiterate, sometimes God's plans don't align with ours, but they're always for the better.

After everything that occurred between Susi and I, I was left with a lot of insecurities and self-doubt but was still determined to fight for our marriage. That fight became our top concern and, without exception, our daily mission. I quickly understood that in order for us to be successful, we needed to rearrange our priorities, change our surroundings, and filter our influences. We knew that most likely I couldn't go back to the comfort and routine of leading worship at the local church that had been such a passion for me for so long.

That decision was only hastened when I found out that just one person from the church had visited Susi during that trying time in her life and that none of her once close friends had reached out to her to see how she was doing or bring her a word of comfort and support in her time of need. That hurt. Those things were out of my control, as everyone does according to his or her conscience and conviction. But it surely left a bad taste in my mouth when I saw how badly they had treated her. In everyone's eyes, including my own, I was the apparent victim in this sad novel that so publicly chronicled the demise of our marriage, and I had reason to be angry at, and harbor bitterness toward, Susi. That being said, I still found it difficult to understand everyone's cold and sanctimonious attitude toward her.

Although God had already instilled it in my heart to make a radical move, letting go and adjusting priorities proved more difficult than I first imagined. The decisive moment arrived in a way that surprised us both. After Susi and I had begun reconnecting, dating consistently for a few weeks, we received an invitation to have dinner at some friends' house. They were a couple from church, and we were excited at the possibility of sharing what God was doing in our lives and hopeful of finding support for the arduous road ahead. They had known us since before we were married, and when we arrived at their house we brought with us high expectations and grateful hearts.

When we finally sat at the table and the conversation began, our joy and excitement soon turned to dejection and disappointment, as we were confronted with the harsh reality and true motive behind the invitation: they weren't in agreement with our getting back together. They gave us several reasons that, for us, were far from the realm of everything we had come to know as being part of God's loving, merciful, and restoring character. They were transparent and blunt, mentioning the timeframe of our union as one of the factors for their conclusion, namely, how they felt it had been too rushed. We politely listened and respectfully disagreed. Voices weren't raised, and no one made a fuss. But the result was immediate and defining. On the outside, it appeared to be any other night with friends, except that the blessing and support we so longed for never arrived.

They never understood how difficult it had been for us just to make it to their house that night as a couple—to sit at their table and open up our hearts, considering the impossible and embracing the supernatural. After all we had been through, just being there was a miracle. They couldn't bring themselves to comprehend that what they were witnessing in that moment right in front of them defied explanation. It couldn't be analyzed with human reason, because it wasn't of this world. It was a God thing.

That night in our car on the way home Susi and I came to the conclusion that what we were embarking on was going to be a lonely journey. God's plans sometimes don't make sense; they forsake analysis and can very well fall out of the scope of what many might consider normal or acceptable. But if it's from God, it will all work out for good. In spite of feeling discouraged and sad after sharing with our friends that night, we reaffirmed our commitment to one another, vowing to continue forward no matter who stood against us.

We were stopped at a light, still close to our friends' house, when something incredible happened that made us fully aware of the magnitude of our decision. After a few minutes the light turned green, and as anyone would normally do, I took my foot off the brakes. As the car began to move forward, something inside told me to stop. No sooner had I done so than a truck passed in front of our car at such a high speed that it shook our vehicle. The driver had run the red light and missed us by inches. We didn't have time to say anything or react in any way, but in that instant we both realized how close we had come to dying. In the span of just milliseconds our story could've ended so differently, and God's plan for our lives would've been buried and forgotten. But the Word of God says:

> *The angel of the Lord encamps around those who fear him, and he delivers them.*

> —PSALM 34:7, NIV

God's plan for our lives was in full effect, and although the enemy would try to destroy, divert, and delay it, nothing anyone could do would impede His destiny for us.

New Priorities and Opportunities

When God opens doors, they simply represent divine opportunities to reach the fulfillment of His purpose for our lives. They are portals through which we can see a glimpse of what can occur when we walk in faith. But in order to reach those desired results, we must modify our way of thinking, change our crossed-arms posture, and begin to take steps forward, entering through those doors with a willingness to embrace the unknown.

The time to break with old patterns and restructure priorities, leaving the safety of our comfort zone to begin walking in faith under God's new purpose, had arrived. I soon realized that the

117

place I called home and where we had fellowshiped for so many years was not where God would have us be restored. We would have to leave behind the nearby and familiar, and welcome the faraway and new, believing in ourselves and trusting in God. It wasn't easy for me since that was the church where I'd served for so long and where all of my friends worshiped. But doing the right thing and what God requires will not always take you down the easy path.

After that night, uniting our hearts in one accord, Susi and I decided we needed to surround ourselves with people who would support and encourage us on this uphill climb we were now embarking upon, understanding it was the best decision for both of us. We eliminated everything and everyone we felt was not going to contribute something positive toward our goal. No mass e-mails were sent out, nor a group text letting people know what we had decided to do. There wasn't a need to assemble a meeting and discuss the matter with our friends, nor have a good-bye party. It was something that occurred on its own. Those who loved us allowed their presence to be felt in our lives, and the rest disappeared without a trace. For a while it seemed as if it was her and I against the world, but in fact, God always went before us, and that made all the difference.

That dinner at our friends' house wasn't the only uncomfortable moment we experienced, not by a long shot. In time, Susi began to frequent the bookstore and would help me run it whenever possible. In years past God had used her to bring words of comfort and hope to customers in need, so it was painful for me to see that now some of them—especially the ones that Susi had helped by sharing both time and advice—were all of a sudden not wanting her to attend to them. When they would walk in the bookstore they would look for me, waving her off with judgment in their eyes. Wherever we went we found people who knew what she had done and, more often than not, would try their hardest to avoid even saying hello, giving her looks of disdain instead. But now she was by my side, and whatever they did to her, they were also doing to me—and none of it was acceptable.

Consequently, the bookstore became a burden for both of us. It no longer was the place of refuge and ministry we so lovingly cultivated for the benefit of the community. It had lost its luster and overstayed its welcome in our lives. But, what could I do if it was my only source of income at the time? I was no longer working at the church; therefore, my only salary came from the bookstore, and it was more ministry than business, barely staying afloat.

That store was all that was left to help me cover living expenses, and it surely wasn't enough. Something had to be done, or I would lose everything. Susi had given me the house in the divorce, but during the bookstore years we took out a second mortgage to invest in inventory and upgrades. That decision was now a financial burden on my life, and drastic changes were needed. Once again my ego had to be put aside.

The first thing that happened was that a friend of mine who had been interested in purchasing the bookstore came by with an offer to buy it. It wasn't much, but it was enough to where it was no longer a financial burden on my life and I could freely pursue God's new purpose for us, this time living by faith. However, this meant that for the time being there was no longer anything I could rely on to supply my financial needs. There was no church salary, no bookstore income, and no more great ideas from Ricardo Rodríguez. Now it was God's turn.

For two years, this friend paid down the bookstore with monthly payments, and those payments were our sole source of income until God's plan was realized in its totality. Still today, I thank God for my friend, who let himself be used by God and was a part of His purpose for our lives.

Nonetheless, the sale of the business still wasn't enough to cover all expenses, so more drastic changes were required. I decided to rent my house, knowing full well it was my only option. I spoke to some family members, and as it turned out, one of Susi's aunts needed a place to live. She went to see the house and rented it right away.

After that, all that was left was figuring out where I would live, since Susi and I were still not yet ready to move back in together. God bless mothers! I mentioned my situation to my mom, and she graciously allowed me to return to her house and live there indefinitely. I won't lie, going back to my mom's house was humbling and embarrassing to say the least. After feeling so independent, having a business, being worship leader of one of the biggest churches in Miami, living in my own house, and living the life of a confident man, here I was back at my mom's house in the same small room I used to sleep in as an adolescent.

With the rental money and the sale on the bookstore I would have barely enough to keep us going for the foreseeable future, but if I was counting pennies before to survive, the belt would have to tightened even further just to make ends meet.

Unscheduled Sabbatical

So there I was again living in my mom's house and Susi still back at her parents. It was a total reset of our lives, but this time we would follow the path God had originally mapped for us. In spite of my commitment to the process, those first few steps of our new life together were, for me, halting and uncomfortable. My life had taken a one hundred eighty-degree turn. At some points it seemed as if I were only taking steps backward, that nothing was going right. But it was all part of God's master plan. There was a process in the works to mold my character, change the characteristics of my heart, and prepare me for the blessing that was to come. Losing everything was humbling, but at the same time it forced me to depend more on His grace and favor. My steps would no longer be ordered by my own wisdom, nor my capacity to be a good administrator. I couldn't have a plan B, a boat on the shore just in case God's plans didn't work out. I had to deposit my full confidence and trust in Him once and for all, walking in faith and obedience.

For the first time in my life I found myself having nothing to do on a Sunday morning. I didn't have a church, and honestly, after having served for so many years in one, faithfully giving my passion, my talent, and my time, I was exhausted and burned out. I needed a break. Ever since the age of twelve I've had some kind of responsibility in church that required me to be present and accounted for. Early on it was as the keyboardist of the church my family and I attended, and finally it was as the worship leader/ music director of a big congregation during my marriage with Susi. Serving God had been my passion from the very promising beginning to the unceremonious end.

It was only when I stepped back that I realized I was tired both physically and emotionally, as the church had taken priority over my well-being and my marriage. Only then could I see that every hour that I had pledged to help and serve somewhere whenever my name was mentioned was an hour Susi never got back with me. The passion I had dedicated to being the best worship leader and music director in church was unwittingly being taken, and never returned, from Susi's rightful share. However, I was determined that things were going to change, and so I decided to take a sabbatical and, for the first time in my life, disconnect from those responsibilities and work only on Susi's and my relationship.

At first I felt super strange waking up on Sunday morning with nowhere to go and nothing to do, but living unburdened from schedules and tasks gave me a sense of freedom I had never experienced. Susi and I began taking long trips alone, making up for lost time and appreciating every minute we shared together. We had been through so much that just getting away from the daily routine and clearing our heads was a vacation to paradise.

Nonetheless, it was clear in our hearts that our desire to receive the Word and share with others of our faith was a real one and needed to be filled. We also knew that, with the help of God, one day we would find a place to gather with believers and be a part of a church again. But after everything we had lived through, we needed a break—and we so enjoyed it. Every once in a while, when we felt the need for a little Pentecostal interaction, we would visit my mom's church, but those were the exceptions. Through it all, God was patient and loving, never allowing us to feel far away from His grace and mercy.

During this season I learned that I didn't need to sing or lead worship for Him to love me, that I could take time to enjoy life without feeling guilty and indebted. It was another level of relationship that I was experiencing, and it changed my way of thinking forever. In hindsight, I see that He never wanted my talent or abilities, nor did He need my loyalty to the ministry. He wasn't going to love me more because I spent all day in church, nor because I sacrificed my dreams and my family. He just wanted me, to be my friend. I finally knew God as someone I could cry to and laugh with, share my dreams and aspirations with, and open up my heart to without the fear of reproach and condemnation. It didn't matter where I went; God would always be by my side.

FIGHTING FOR SURVIVAL

Susi and I continued crossing that cruel and difficult desert that would punish us without mercy physically, emotionally, and spiritually. There were OK days and terrible days, and at moments it all felt hopeless and without merit. But it smelled like summer rain, and in the distance we could see a cloud of blessings quickly approaching.

We began to visit a marriage counselor who helped us get through the rough patches and align our focus toward the end result. He was someone far from our circle of friends, someone who knew nothing about us but above all was a believer. He breathed words of life into our marriage with his wise counsel and guidance and helped me deal with my anger and self-control issues.

Susi and I wanted to be together, and we fought long and hard through hell and high water to make it so. We put aside our friends and family, our business, and whatever else we felt was going to be a hindrance just to regain what we had lost. It wasn't easy, it wasn't quick, and it wasn't free—but it was worth the price, the time, and the sacrifice. Like everything in life, we understood that to achieve great results, mediocre efforts wouldn't suffice. It was all or nothing, and no one would steal our victory. Everything we had to do in order to reach our goal we were more than willing to do.

Chapter 8

I'LL KEEP ON SINGING

by Ricardo Rodríguez

I'VE ALWAYS BEEN immensely grateful for the faith my mother and grandmother instilled in me as a child, but I have come to appreciate the care and attention they invested to train me up in the ways of the Lord more with every passing day. They raised me with the fear of God firmly anchored in my heart and the certainty that He never fails. It didn't matter how difficult the situation or impossible the problem might be; He was always the first and only option. That seed of faith that was sown years before bore fruit in the most opportune moment of my life.

What I went through could have easily been a death sentence, or at least destroyed my emotional state forever. Drugs, alcohol, illicit relationships—they were all easily accessible vices I could've used to help alleviate the depression and pain I was experiencing at the time. These are very common recourses, and sometimes on my worst days when I was swallowing those bitter tears and dealing with the pain of Susi's betrayal I perfectly understood why some get caught up in those types of traps. But every time I felt motivated to use my crisis as an excuse to try something out of God's will and possibly ease the hurt, I remembered my mother's words. Thankfully, I knew those alternatives could never provide a path to real healing and the restoration of my emotions, my heart, and ultimately, my marriage. I crossed that desert with God's help—and the prayers and guiding words of my mom and grandma.

*Start children off on the way they should go, and
even when they are old they will not turn from it.*

—PROVERBS 22:6, NIV

INSPIRED AND IMPASSIONED

My first attempts at songwriting were as a member of Newlife. It all started with a challenge from one of the guys to do more than just covers as a band. We wanted something new and fresh that would give a defining identity to the group and somehow help us be relevant. I was seventeen years old and had never written anything, but that didn't deter me from accepting the challenge and beginning to pen my first lines as a songwriter.

I recall the first song I submitted to the band. It was titled "Guided by the Light," and I was nervous and excited to show the guys. I presented it in one of the rehearsals, and we quickly began to arrange it. The positive reaction motivated me to continue writing, and so in the next rehearsal I brought my second song, "On Behalf of Jesus." This one caused a definite stir in the room as soon as I played it. It was a weird and different sensation for me seeing the smile on their faces and hearing the surprise and admiration in the comments afterward.

On a sidenote, I wasn't always the lead singer of the group. On many occasions during rehearsals I would put a microphone on the piano and, without asking, would try to sing backup on some of the songs. The effort was never well received. The band director's immediate response was always, "Concentrate on the piano and leave the microphone alone." Therefore, when I received approval and support after they heard my songs, I was truly motivated and inspired to continue down this new endeavor that continues to be my calling and passion even today. Once a timid and soft-spoken young man with a paralyzing fear of speaking in public, suddenly there I was center stage with a platform to share what God had put in my heart. It was amazing. Composing became an all-consuming exercise that took up most of my time and dedication. Looking back during that period with Newlife, I'm grateful that God birthed many songs through me, which ultimately led us to record three albums.

Later on, though, after Susi and I were married, I put aside that gift that God had bestowed upon me. At first I thought it would be temporary, but my priorities changed, and the time and passion required for writing never returned to me. Many years passed without me writing or recording anything significant and worthwhile.

It wasn't until my life—which had been going one hundred miles per hour—crashed spectacularly into the wall that was the failure of my marriage that things finally began to change. Yes, I was unemployed and living again with my mother, but there during that stressful and life-altering crisis, the piano and the desire to write became a priority once more. Instead of trying to ease my pain by going out with friends on weekends or getting lost in a world of codependency, I would hide in my poems and my songs. It was my drug of choice.

I remember, when we had the bookstore there was a small room in the back where I would spend hours working on melodies and lyrics. It was a space that only fit myself and the piano. It wasn't fancy, and it didn't have sophisticated equipment, but God was always present. There He would speak to me, and it was there where I reconnected with the gift that had once brought so much joy to my life. Again, it was God's perfect plan. When we sold the bookstore, my mother's living room took over as that special place of refuge and inspiration.

It was in those two places that some of my most popular songs were written. I wrote because it gave me comfort and would ease my pain and because it was my passion and my calling, but most of all, I wrote because it drew me closer to God. Hearing His voice was what I longed for the most. Every line of every song that came from my heart spoke about His faithfulness, His love and forgiveness, and His healing and restoring power.

In obeying God and forgiving Susi, I felt the floodgates of inspiration and anointing open up and, like a rushing river, begin to pour over me. God had deposited His heart in mine, and like a pen in His hands, I once again felt useful and filled with purpose. He would awaken me in the evening and inspire me by day. I recall one of those late nights/early mornings hearing a voice speak to my heart. Throughout the years God had always spoken to me at all hours of the night to inspire me with melodies and lyrics, and I was familiar with His voice. On that night it was almost three o'clock when I heard Him clearly say, "Keep on singing." All of a sudden, the lyrics came pouring down from heaven and into my heart as I frantically scrambled for something to write on.

> I'll keep on singing,
> for You are the God of miracles,
> Sovereign and faithful,
> Lord and King of my life.
>
> I give You praise,
> For my hope comes from above.
> If it's my turn to lose,
> I'll never ask why.
> Lord, let Your will be done.
> My life is in your hands.

It profoundly moved me as soon as I heard it. They were incredible lyrics with a moving melody that I knew had to write down quickly before I could forget it. There were no smartphones or iPads during that time, and I had no recording device easily accessible to save this jewel God had given me. So in the dim light of the wee hours I opened up the nightstand drawer and reached in for the first piece of paper I could find. Half asleep and trying hard not to forget any word, I quickly wrote down the lyrics on the back of those papers. When I finished, feeling satisfied and thankful, I laid my head down and fell soundly asleep.

The next day when I awoke, the first thing I did was reach for those papers on which I had written down this gift from heaven. Now with the morning sun shining bright I could clearly see what I had written, but just as importantly, I could see where it was written. I couldn't believe my eyes! It was the divorce papers! The same pages that had once represented so much pain and failure in my life had now been transformed into a symbol of hope and possibility through the lyrics of this song. One side held the death sentence for my marriage, and the other, the heart of a man full of hope and faith, unwilling to bow down and accept such a decree.

The song shouted out that God was still God, and that even in the darkest moment of life, when all seems lost, He can make a way. In that moment I realized that God wasn't going to let a good piece of paper go to waste, and that even from the ashes of our marriage He was going to birth something beautiful! It was only the beginning, but every step was promising and exciting. Something new was pouring down from heaven over my life, and without a doubt, it would change my destiny.

God's Provision on Its Way

I was inspired during that season of my life and couldn't stop writing. One song after another was born in a period of just a few weeks, and I knew that God was behind each one. I wrote without ever planning to record or even sing them live. It was simply a way of unburdening myself and letting God know what was on my heart.

At the time, the only two people who heard my songs were Susi and a good friend named Isaac Hernandez. They were my soundboards and test subjects whenever I felt inspired and needed feedback and affirmation. Susi was always telling me how beautiful they were and how I needed to record them ASAP. She never had a negative thing to say about my efforts and was always willing to listen to whatever crazy musical ideas would pop up in my head, no matter the time or place. From the start, she demonstrated more faith in me than I had in myself, inspiring me to continue writing and not simply to conclude that my songs were to be used only for our personal enjoyment. Recording wasn't on the radar though, and even if it had been, I couldn't have afforded to record half a song with my finances being what they were.

I'd met Isaac working on Newlife projects years before. He was, and continues to be, a great producer and the brother I never had. From the very beginning he was a firm believer in my abilities and continues to be one of my closest confidants. We've worked together on all seventeen of my solo albums, so suffice it to say, my admiration for him and his musical genius has only grown since our first collaboration with Newlife back in 1988. He's always seemed to know how to bring out the best in me with motivating words and constructive criticism. In the studio he would push me far beyond what I thought my vocal capabilities were. In his mind I had limitless potential. Isaac always told me I had the unique talent to sing any genre and impressed in me not to be afraid of getting out of my comfort zone and trying different things. He taught me to believe in my talent and to trust in what God had deposited in my hands and in my heart. His advice was always wise and encouraging, but at the same time, he wouldn't hesitate to confront me when he felt it was warranted. Through him I learned that true friends don't hide the truth; they keep it real and aren't afraid to lose a friendship on account of integrity and openness.

I will say that every time I would send him a new song or idea, looking for his opinion and advice, it was an adventure and an ego check, to say the least. His comments were always blunt and unfiltered but never without direction and positive reinforcement. Every once in awhile though, I would surprise him with something unexpected that would leave him speechless, and it was fun. One of those moments was with the song "Quizás Hoy" (Maybe Today). On the day I played it for him I was working with him in the studio on background vocals for another artist. (I did many background vocals for other artists during that time to help make ends meet.) During one of the breaks I told him, "I have something new. Give me your opinion," and I began to sing it *a capella*. When I finished I noticed him silent, and I'm pretty sure I even saw a tear or two being wiped away. Anxiously I asked, "What do you think?" But he couldn't talk. It was a hit!

That song wound up being used by the Billy Graham Evangelistic Association in several Latin American Crusades, where millions of people heard it and, through the power of the Holy Spirit, were impacted and moved to give their lives to Jesus. Based on the story of the prodigal son—but from the point of view of the father— it still brings me to tears today. I cannot play it without thinking of the night God laid it on my heart and the transformation that came with it. That night when I surrendered to His will and the work He wanted to do in me and in my relationship with Susi, I prayed that God would allow someone to be impacted and blessed by the painful process I had endured. In the end, God kept His end of the bargain, and "Quizás Hoy" is one of the many tools He has used for that purpose. Any time I see the Spirit of God use that song to confront, heal, and restore hearts, I'm reminded that He never fails.

After showing Isaac "Quizás Hoy" that night, I was motivated to continue writing, and once I had enough songs, I shared with him my desire to record again. Of course, I didn't mention that fact I had no money; I left that part till the end. But after hearing the songs, he told me, "The time is now. These songs are incredible, and you have to share them with the world." They were the words I needed to hear. He mentioned there was a record label that was looking for a new artist to sign and that he would definitely recommend me. I couldn't believe it! Could it be that after all I had suffered and lost, there was actually a chance I could be signed by a major label and record my songs for the world to hear? I would have to wait two more years before the answer to that question would arrive.

While the label took their time in deciding who to sign, God had clearly spoken to me and confirmed that I needed to do the best I could with the resources I had, and that's just what I did. I committed myself to continuing to develop myself personally and professionally, refusing to become stagnant in the process of transformation God was working in me and in my relationship with Susi. That journey was far from easy, but it has always been worth it.

Sometimes we become so focused on what our eyes see and our minds can process that these perceptions turn into excuses and obstacles that wind up blocking God's purpose for our lives. We need to be reminded that we serve a God who requires faith for His hand to move and who always glorifies Himself in our scarcity. After all, He fed the multitude with two fish and five loaves of bread, turned the water into wine at the wedding of Cana, and didn't allow the widow at Zarephath to run out of oil. What won't He do for you? He's still that same miracle-provoking, supernatural-manifesting, always on time, and never failing God today that He was yesterday! And He is always looking to turn the broken and discarded into priceless vessels of honor for His glory.

WEDDING BELLS

Susi and I were seeing each another more often with each passing day. Every step we took forward was taking us one step farther from our past and the painful memories associated with it and one step closer to the fulfillment of God's promise for our marriage. After a year of dating and marital counseling, I felt in my heart it was the right time for us to celebrate our new beginning with a renewed commitment to one another. One day, taking her hand in my mine, I asked the question she so longed to hear: "What if we start over?" She glanced at me with tears in her eyes and responded, "Together till the end."

There weren't many invited guests, nor was there a huge party thrown. No one brought gifts, and the ceremony was as simple and short as could be. But without a doubt, that day was one of the best days of our lives. Standing face to face, two hopeful hearts in one accord, we got to see firsthand the restoring power that exists when repentance meets forgiveness. It was a new beginning, ushering in another level of relationship and also of ministry. With God's help, there would be no looking back, as we were confident that the best was yet to come.

We continued living between my mom's and my in-laws' houses. Our home had been rented out and was at the time unavailable, but our families were gracious and beyond helpful, opening their doors without questions or pretexts.

By then I was also working in local studios doing background vocals to make ends meet. The income helped, but I knew God had something more in store for me. Nevertheless, I embraced that season of my life, looking at it as part of the preparation for what lay ahead—and enjoying every minute of it. I got the opportunity to work with well-known artists in the Spanish secular market and alongside the best of the best in the studio doing vocals. They helped me hone my craft, motivating me to reach new heights of vocal technique and helping improve my confidence along the way.

Susi and I had been getting by on my sparse income, and although we didn't live wanting, it was difficult sometimes. Living off of God's provision was a day-to-day exercise, but we can both testify that He never failed. My world, although still small, slowly and carefully began expanding, and once again I started to deposit my trust in those around me.

BRANCHING OUT AS A SOLOIST

Although I was routinely using my voice in the studio in and around Miami, I hadn't sung in front of a congregation or anywhere else publicly in quite a while. This made it all the more surprising when one day I received a call from an old friend, one I hadn't seen or spoken to in years, who made me a compelling offer. He asked me how things were going, and not wanting to dig up my past, I focused on the present and responded with positive and glowing reviews of my new life. He told me about a concert he was organizing in his city and explained that he wanted me to open up for him if I was available. I was shocked, speechless really. I wasn't a soloist and didn't have a recording to promote, nor any songs prepared to sing live. I lived in anonymity in my protective bubble and couldn't offer him anything of value to enhance and/or promote his concert.

We knew each other back in my Newlife days, and although we hadn't kept in touch throughout the years, we had a mutual respect and affinity for each other's talents. Nonetheless, I knew he could've easily invited anyone to be a part of this grand event. "Why me?" I asked, incredulous. He simply responded, "I'd been praying over who to bring to the concert, and God put you on my heart. So don't delay in making a decision, because God is waiting." Wow! This was a supernatural gift from above, and I couldn't say no. With a tremble in my voice and butterflies in my stomach, I answered that yes, I would do it, not even knowing what songs I would sing. He suggested I do some of my old Newlife songs, which had ministered to him so much in the past, and definitely to not forget his favorite, "Espera en Mí" (Wait on Me).

That concert was my first experience singing as a soloist, standing alone on stage and finally stepping out of my comfort zone. It was there I first saw God's plan for my life begin to take flight.

That friend's name was René González, and that trip to Puerto Rico for the concert marked a before-and-after in my life and the beginning of my solo music ministry. Rene is still a great friend, one to whom I'm deeply grateful and will always be indebted.

Soon after my trip to Puerto Rico I received a call from one of the biggest and most influential churches in El Salvador. I couldn't believe it. Why hadn't these invitations arrived before? Why now, when I most needed it, were these people and churches calling? I wasn't marketing myself and didn't have a publicist or a label; nobody knew me, but yet God was opening doors in a supernatural way. Elim Church in El Salvador wanted me to be a part of their six services on Sunday, where close to thirty-six thousand congregants faithfully attended. My first solo presentation had been just a few weeks back, and now I was being asked to fly to a country I had never visited and sing in front of thousands of people. Again I asked, Why me? (This was my favorite question at the time.) They let me know that Newlife's music had been a blessing and was beloved in the congregation, and to them it would be an honor to have the lead singer share those songs and lead them in worship. I said yes and let them know I would need two plane tickets.

The brethren from Elim Church blessed our lives tremendously, treating us with great love, graciousness, and respect. Susi and I needed to feel appreciated at that juncture in our lives, and God delivered abundantly. It was also amazing to hear thousands of people sing my songs with so much fervor and commitment. Unbeknownst to me, those songs had become church favorites that were sung almost every Sunday in Elim. Both Susi and myself returned home amazed, grateful, and assured that what God had planned for us would surpass even our greatest expectations. We understood that the future for us consisted of travel and ministry, commitment and sacrifice, but we also knew we would be doing it together.

Those trips to Puerto Rico and El Salvador motivated me to pursue the idea of getting back in the studio and finally recording my solo project. I had the songs, the best producer to arrange them, and a green light from God. All that was left was figuring out where to get the financing. Isaac proposed an idea that at first glance seemed absurd to me. He knew full well I couldn't afford to record the album of my dreams and the one my songs deserved, so instead of waiting around for a label to sign me, he suggested I record an album of old songs, like the ones I grew up singing as child in church. It would fall within my meager budget, be easy and quick to record, and provide me with a product to have for future presentations. With God's help, I could record my original compositions later on and have a proper solo album.

In reality, it wasn't a new concept. Years before, I had produced a similar album for the church, but I hated the idea. The thought of redoing songs from my youth (and with Caribbean rhythms nonetheless) didn't appeal to me, and I fought it every step of the way. I saw it as dated and old fashioned and kept thinking about all the effort I had put into writing my own songs. I wanted to do originals, and he was proposing covers my grandma used to sing. I found the whole idea humiliating. I gave him a million excuses, but in the end, God was going to give me another lesson in humility and obedience.

AND THE MOUNTAIN SHALL BE MOVED

Putting my ego aside, Isaac and I went into the studio and began to record. In 1999 I launched the first two productions of *Alabanzas del Pueblo* (Praises From the People), volumes 1 and 2, and even though at first I was vehemently opposed to the idea, the process of recording changed my mind. It turned out to be an amazing experience. First, just being able to record with Isaac once again after so many years did me good. Second, those songs blessed my life more than I could ever explain. Recording them took me back to my early years in church, reminding me of a simpler time and how my love of music began. They profoundly moved me and everyone involved in the recording process.

On the other hand, I had never distributed music and found it extremely intimidating and challenging. I recall how scared and insecure Susi and I felt on the day we drove to pick up the first batch of cassettes we had made. It was an investment we couldn't afford in an industry we didn't fully understand, but it was too late to change our minds, and there was too much at stake to simply fail. We would not be backing down from the challenge. That being said, it was only when we arrived at home and began to stack the boxes in the office that the full magnitude of the situation began to sink in. The mountain of cassettes reached the ceiling and practically filled the whole room. What were we thinking? How were we going to sell all this product? I had no idea!

All of a sudden I remembered everything that had occurred in that same room not more than two years before. On that fateful night I had received a heartbreaking confession from my wife, and I walked out of that office destroyed and hopeless, thinking everything was finished. It seemed at the time that our dreams and aspirations died there, and whatever hope we shared of living a happily married life as husband and wife were burned at the altar of betrayal and resentment in that very spot. That room represented many sleepless nights and all the anger, anguish, and shame Susi and I endured. For a long time it stood as a symbol of all the worst parts of our marriage. But after everything we'd gone through, after crossing that unforgiving desert of despair, there we stood once again by the grace of God, contemplating our future together. I knew that if God had done a miracle in our marriage, there wasn't a mountain of boxes on Earth that could impede His purpose from being fulfilled and His blessings from pouring down on our lives. He hadn't brought us this far to leave us short.

Therefore, with trusting and grateful hearts, we lifted a prayer: "Lord, we are here by Your grace and mercy, standing together as one because You have allowed it. We thank You for what You've done and for all that You are about to do. Just as our lives are in Your hands, so are these humble offerings we now lay before You.

Do with them as You please and according to Your perfect will. Glorify Yourself in each song and bless all those who sow in this fledgling ministry with the purchase of one of these albums."

The next day I called various distributors in Puerto Rico that Isaac knew and had recommended. Soon after, we were sending demos of our productions to see if anyone was interested in selling them. All that was left after that was to patiently wait and trust on the Lord.

To our dismay and disillusion, only one distributor responded positively. His name was Benjamin Rivera, and in our conversation with him, he let us know he felt the concept and interpretation were different than anything presently in the market and that with the right marketing it was something he could get behind. He made a small order with the promise of taking it to the radio stations in Puerto Rico and getting in touch with us again in a few weeks. But weeks passed, and nothing happened. Every time the phone rang my heart would skip a beat. I recall many times seeing the mountain of cassettes as I passed by the office and feeling as though they were mocking me. But our faith was resolute, and we continued to believe that God had everything under control.

On the third week we received the long-awaited call. Benjamín Rivera needed more music! A week after that, another distributor called. Though at first he didn't have any interest in our product, he also placed an order. We couldn't believe what was going on! In less than two months that mountain of music had disappeared. God had glorified Himself in an amazing way, and in doing so gave me another valuable lesson that even today I apply in all my endeavors: Your faith will always take you farther than what your resources and capabilities can promise.

Out of all the productions I've had the blessing of releasing throughout my life, *Alabanzas del Pueblo* (Praises From the People), now in Volumes 1 through 5, continue to be some of our best and most beloved sellers. Those humble recordings that were done with scarce resources—but with an abundance of love—have touched the lives of millions of people and were the means by which God lifted us out of that burden of debt left hanging over our heads after the divorce.

In six months we were able to accomplish what in four years we had struggled to do: be debt free. I had put my talent aside for fear of failure, always falling back into the comfort of the secure and tangible and trusting in my own wisdom and strength to attain financial freedom. It never arrived. It was only when I surrendered to God's will and perfect plan, putting aside my fears, that the heavens opened up and blessings began to pour down. I didn't have to fight for them; they arrived on their own. I didn't turn my back on my calling or my talents to reach them. Just being myself was sufficient. There weren't any marketing strategies, nor sophisticated sales techniques involved. It was just accomplished through an obedience to His Word, an embracing of His will, and a surrendering to His original plan. I never could've imagined in that moment that it was just the tip of the iceberg of what God had in store for us.

Many times for blessings to reach our lives God waits until every accessible resource, earthly provision, and human scheme has been thoroughly exhausted. It is there when looking around and finding no other alternative but to trust in Him that the manna from heaven begins to come down and He manifests Himself in our lives as Jehovah Jireh, our Provider. He does it so we can look up, recognizing that it was never by our strength but by His power and for His glory.

MINISTERIAL GROWTH

Soon after, the opportunity that we'd been waiting for, for two years arrived: the chance to sign with the label that would allow us to record the album we had always dreamed of. Excited and with high expectations, we went into the studio and began to develop the ideas that would make my songs sound like I'd always hoped they would.

As the days rolled on and the work progressed, I began to notice there was something supernatural going on with the production. Isaac, being the consummate professional he was, put in the effort and dedication required to polish my songs and make them sound magnificent. As I listened to the playback of the different cuts, I was overcome. Every song echoed a piece of my heart, making palpable all I had gone through, and thanks to God and Isaac, it was all captured on the recording. Sometimes with tears in our eyes and knots in our throats, but always with passion and devotion, we managed to make it to the end. As we wrapped up the recording, we knew we had something special in our hands.

The album *Mi Deseo* (My Desire) was released in the year 2000 under the WORD LATIN label, and with the launching of that production we saw another one of our dreams become reality. It quickly climbed the sales charts and wound up being the number-one selling Hispanic album for WORD that year, and God's favor continued to be poured over our lives and ministry. Not long after, the video for the single "Quizás Hoy" (Maybe Today) was also released, and that took everything to another level.

Witnessing the effect of that song in so many lives, sometimes in the simple shedding of a tear and at others through the Spirit-lead surrendering of a shattered heart to Jesus, has given me great satisfaction throughout the years. Every time I see the impact it has on the broken, hopeless, forsaken, and unforgiving, I'm reminded of God's promise the night I was inspired to write it. I can testify now that with every tear I shed during that life-altering season I had to endure, God has comforted, healed, and blessed countless souls, restoring hearts and relationships along the way and instilling hope in those who are still waiting for their miracle to arrive.

I'll never forget when I returned to Puerto Rico, this time with my first recording in hand, and appeared at a massive outdoor concert at the invitation of one of the local radio stations. They were gracious enough to invite me to share the stage with many respected and well-established artists who I had admired for so long, and I felt honored. I recall as I opened up the event how nervous I was—and at the same time excited—to share my new songs for the first time, one of them being "Quizás Hoy". It was exhilarating to see the audience's reaction as they heard my compositions, and when I finished, all I could do was praise God for the opportunity and once again stand amazed at how far He had brought me.

As I stood around trying to listen to the rest of the concert and get a glimpse of my favorite artist, a man came up to me with tears in his eyes, looking desperate and distraught. His voice began to tremble when he asked, "Were you the young man who sang the song about the father?" I answered yes, and he continued, "You have no idea how you've touched me with that song, nor what God has just done in my life. This afternoon I had an argument with my fifteen-year-old son, and I threw him out of the house. I don't even remember what the fight was about, but God confronted me as I heard you sing, and right now I'm leaving to go find him and ask him to forgive me. I need to hug my boy and let him know how much I love him." That night, after having paid for a concert that had barely begun, that father decided his son was more important than any artist or event he could ever attend, and being moved by the Holy Spirit, left in search of his boy. Wow! I couldn't believe what God had done! How could a simple song move the heart of a man in such a way that it motivated him to take such drastic measures?

It was obvious to me that it wasn't the song that made the impact, nor my voice or the accompanying music. It was God's supernatural anointing deposited over those lyrics that made all the difference in that man's life. I understood then that the price paid to write those lyrics had been well worth it. The process I had to endure for the message to be valid and real—first for me, but more importantly now for the world—had been a necessary one. It brought transparency and genuineness to my ministry, and I would never write the same again.

Composing to simply sell albums wasn't enough. Creating music for the sake of having radio hits wouldn't suffice. Remembering my process and understanding God's purpose for my life, more than anything, has made me focus on being an instrument of inspiration in His hands every time I sit down to write. It is my sincere desire to be vessel of honor where His anointing can pour out into the lives around me through my music and my life.

If I somehow had the opportunity to go back and change anything about that painful process I went through, I would leave it all as it was. I didn't understand the plan; that was impossible in the middle of the struggle. But God, from the start, had that song in mind—and many others. The only question was in whom He would deposit it. Who would be willing to pay the price, accepting the challenge to see it through to the end until His purpose was fulfilled? It was only one song, but behind it was the profound and real story of forgiveness and mercy filled with rejection and disdain, sleepless nights of bitter desperation, and unrelenting pain. But without that trial—and the redemption that followed—it couldn't have been written.

Praise God for the trials that challenge us, the storms that wash away our manmade dreams and illusions, and the deserts that appear to be our inevitable demise, because through them, God reveals Himself! He shows up in the nick of time as the sovereign God He is, always ready to save, heal, and restore, no matter the impossibility of the circumstance, for our blessing and His glory!

Chapter 9

THE GREAT I AM

by Susana Rodríguez

RICARDO'S MUSIC MINISTRY had begun to take flight, making our ever-changing weekend schedules increasingly hectic and unpredictable. But as long as we were together, I didn't mind. We visited many countries and met countless wonderful people along the way. It was an incredible time of new discovery and personal growth, and without a doubt, it was great for my well-being and self-esteem.

In spite of the healing God had worked in me, sin had left behind many insecurities and fears, and although I understood the importance of overcoming the guilt and shame associated with my transgressions, the road to self-confidence and personal pride had been slow and winding. But in those faraway places no one noticed the pain still hiding behind my smile, nor the shame that every once in while made its unwanted appearance in the most inopportune moments. Traveling the world and living out of a suitcase while sharing ministerial duties with Ricardo helped me find purpose and a new and clear perspective on life in those first years. Slowly but surely, God would work His healing miracle in our lives, and those trips were an important part of that process and just what the doctor ordered.

God's blessings and favor were always upon us, and His unfailing love was a guiding light during those uncertain and shaky first steps of our marriage and ministry. This gave us the assurance we needed to step into the unknown, walking in faith and with purpose as we embraced His call.

During that season we learned to avoid at all costs positioning ourselves once again in vulnerable territory. We strove to keep our priorities straight and our focus on doing His will, but even so, in the years that followed not everything was perfect, as we encountered obstacles and painful situations that once gain tested our resolve and commitment to one another. It would become clear to us that the battles are never over, that we would have to live in a constant state of vigilance and accountability, and that it is essential to learn from past mistakes to avoid repeating them. But most importantly, if there is anything our story demonstrates and that we've learned throughout the years, it is that true love conquers all. It is unconditional, fearless, and bold and will never be defeated when joined by the likes of forgiveness, grace, and mercy.

THE DEEPEST OF YEARNINGS

As Ricardo and I started to pick up the pieces of our broken marriage, cautiously walking forward into our new life together, we both understood it would take our combined strength and determination to make our house a home again. That same effort put forth when we first bought our hurricane-damaged house years before would now have to be applied to the task at hand in order to bring joy, peace, and trust to our badly shattered relationship. It was difficult, sometimes painful, and took time, but the results it yielded made it all worthwhile. Piece by piece, we began to rebuild. So many people had told us our relationship would never emerge from the rubble and ashes, but God had given us a better promise, and we were following His lead.

We could clearly see God's faithfulness and goodness ushering us forward into our complete restoration with every step we took. An hour void of tears and shouting became a day, which later turned into a week and then a month until, with God's help and plenty of therapy, patience, and the moral support of our devoted family, we reached a once seemingly unattainable goal: a loving marriage where trust once again had a place to call home.

But as time passed, it became more and more evident that something was still missing. Even with all the amazing, radical changes that our lives were constantly experiencing and with all the success that we had attained by the grace of God, an emptiness remained that no one or nothing could fill, something that persisted and grew more intense with every passing year—a void that only a child could fill. We serve a God that delights in giving us His best, always granting us the desires of our hearts according to His perfect will. My dream to be a mother, even during that tumultuous time, had remained strong in my heart, and it grew even more when things began to normalize in our relationship.

Still, the years were stacking up, and so were the questions. And the doubts? The doubts were constant and growing more and more with each Mother's Day that passed without me being able to embrace my miracle. Even so, we continued clinging to God's promises and occupying ourselves in the ministry while trying somehow to forget and deny how much we truly needed that gift in our lives. I never stopped dreaming though—dreaming of that unmistakable song heard only in the laughter of a joyful child, of that tender and sincere embrace that would one day melt all my sadness away, and of that moment when expectation would meet reality.

One of the first trips Ricardo and I took together was to the beautiful country of El Salvador. There I met a wonderful woman of God who, just like me, hadn't been able to have children. I asked her how she was able to live a life full of joy and contentment while missing out on the blessing of having a family of her own. Her wise response surprised and deeply touched me: "I'm happy because I have many spiritual children," she said, "I take care of them by showing God's love and offering hope, encouragement, and compassion until they can stand on their own two feet. My days and nights are filled with thankfulness for what I have, never focusing on what is not in God's plan for my life." She was letting me know I needed to lay down all my dreams and my heart's desires at the altar of God's will. I had to prepare myself to accept whatever He had in store for me, whether or not it fit within my well-structured plans and preconceived ideas of how my life should be.

I returned home from that trip meditating on what I'd learned. What would my destiny hold? What purpose would God have for me? I still felt strongly I would be a mother one day, and Ricardo and I, in our many travels, had encountered numerous people who were praying for that very miracle, some of whom even prophesied that it would happen soon. But before we knew it, fifteen years had passed, and the window of opportunity was quickly closing.

When I turned thirty-seven, the doctors, seeing my desperate situation and how time was running out, began to offer me medical solutions and last-resort options to get pregnant. It was all very confusing and overwhelming, leaving me anxious and afraid. But before speaking to Ricardo about what the doctors were proposing to me at the time, I went to God in prayer. I needed to speak to my heavenly Father and feel His peace before any decision would be made, especially one that required medical intervention with potentially life-altering repercussions.

Resolute, I entered my war room and closed the door, saying to myself, "I'm not leaving here without an answer from God!" There, alone with my despairing heart and longing soul, I laid all my hopes and dreams before my heavenly Father, but above all, my profound yearning to be a mother someday. In that moment the story of Hannah came to mind and how her relentless and passionate prayer to have a child was so heart-wrenching and full of anguish that at first even the prophet Eli thought she was drunk. What profound and moving words could she have uttered that somehow provoked the hand of the Father to grant her what she so desired? That's who I wanted to be, what I needed to become—a woman drunk in prayer like Hannah, pouring herself out completely so that God could see and feel the pain in her heart and be moved to respond.

I spent many hours in that room in profound conversation with God, opening up my heart and sharing my deepest and most heartfelt desires but also thanking Him for yesterday's blessings, today's provision, and tomorrow's miracle. In the end, with peace in my heart and clarity in my mind, I walked out of that room confident that God's will for me was to be a mom someday. All that was left was for Ricardo to be on board. Although we had been diagnosed with unexplained infertility, I was at an age that complicated matters, and the promise seemed to be taking the scenic road to reach our lives, I knew that the One who is never late would arrive right on time with our miracle in tow.

A few days passed after my war-room breakthrough, and without me mentioning a word, Ricardo said to me one morning, "I feel in my heart from God that we should speak to the doctor about medical treatments in our pursuit of having children. I'm not sure what the process is, but we should ask him about it and see what steps need to be taken to make our dream a reality. What do you think?" I felt my heart stop beating for a second! I had asked God, if it was His will, to place that same passion I was feeling in Ricardo's heart, and now, just like that, he was confirming it. We were in one accord to proceed with medical treatment, something that for years we saw as being out of our financial reach. But God aligned everything, placing in our hands the resources required and preparing us spiritually, emotionally, and physically for what was to come.

When we spoke to our doctor, he clearly let us know there would be no guarantees the treatment would work. He explained that a high percentage of couples who try IVF don't get pregnant, having to repeat the treatment several times, and even then some never reach their desired goal of having children.

That being said, Ricardo and I were convinced and more willing than ever to do everything possible and necessary to make our dream come true. I recall the day we started sitting in the waiting room with other hopeful and anxious women. Some of them shared with me their many grueling and heartbreaking experiences, telling me not to get my hopes up, as the odds were not in my favor. I always responded with a smile on my face and a declaration of faith in my heart, "My God is the master of impossibilities, and I know He will fulfill His promise in me."

GETTING READY FOR THE MIRACLE

One day I decided to put my faith in action and called my dad with a proposal. Inviting him to our house, I took him upstairs to a room that had always been empty, and there, with optimism and hopefulness, I told him, "Dad, I'd like you to help me paint this room and get it ready for the baby that will soon arrive."

I'll never forget the look on his face, one of confusion with a side of pity. He tried desperately to avoid my stare, searching for a way to escape the uncomfortable conversation, and didn't say a word. His silence, though, spoke volumes. He was well aware we'd been trying a long time to have children and had seen our frustrations throughout the years, so in asking him for this favor, I can only imagine he must have thought, "What is this poor child doing preparing a room for a baby when she's not even pregnant?" Even so, wanting to please his daughter's hopeful heart, he began to paint that abandoned room. For two days he went over every nook and cranny of that empty space with his brush with detail and precision until finally, when he was all done, it was worthy of a picture in a magazine. (My father had been a painter for many years.) All the time he worked in that room, he remained silent. But his face couldn't mask the conflict and worry he was carrying within.

In the meantime, I continued believing God. When the painting was finished, I quickly began to fill the room with all things baby and some hopes and dreams for good measure. Ricardo, stepping into faith himself, also got involved, and one day arrived with a small baby blanket, a gesture that made me burst out crying uncontrollably. But these were no longer tears of pain and sorrow. No, this time around, thankfulness and joy took the reins and made their presence felt. I knew God had something special for both of us and that soon His promise would be fulfilled.

Ricardo and I had gone through so much together—turbulent seas of pain and anguish, angry storms of resentment and bitterness, and that cruel and lonely desert of our separation and subsequent divorce—but in the end, with God's help, we stood stronger than ever. Now, this new miracle was drawing near, and the moment was ours to enjoy!

The IVF treatment, on the other hand, was difficult both emotionally and physically. I had to prepare my body and mind for what they were about to embark upon. But I was determined and confident and more than ever assured that God was in the middle of it all. Just as the physical aspect of the process had been covered by the doctors and their medicines, the spiritual side of it all was also being taken care of by the many prayers of friends, family members, and of course Ricardo. It was all placed at the feet of the almighty God, knowing He had everything under control.

The doctors did an amazing job calming my fears and anxieties. During every visit and exam, and with each injection and sometimes painful procedure, I felt reassured and hopeful it would all be a success. Ricardo, my best friend and confidant, didn't miss a single doctor's visit, and his words of encouragement and faith gave me the strength necessary to reach the finish line.

There were many visits to the doctor, and in every one of them I would daydream the hours away. Those dreams were always filled with visions of a baby girl. For some reason God had put it on my heart that we would have a girl and that she would look just like me, all the way from her long braids to her beautiful smile. I would spend my days and nights visualizing every detail of her beautiful, tiny face. It was a wonderful time in our lives, full of well-deserved happiness.

One day Ricardo and I arrived early to see the doctor and discuss the final details of the crucial moment when everything would be decided. He explained with patience and precise detail that the following day would be the most important one of the whole three-month ordeal. I needed to have a good night's sleep and arrive early in the morning with zero stress and a peaceful mind-set. He let us know that everything was now riding on my body's ability to accept the treatment, and as we left, he once again reiterated the importance of resting and being of calm mind and spirit when we returned the next morning. The time had come. Everything was ready! All the effort and sacrifice had led us to this life-altering moment, and with God's help it would be a success.

Returning home that day, once again we presented our doubts and concerns before God in prayer, declaring that our son or daughter would serve Him with all their heart and that we would do our best to guide him, with the help of the Holy Spirit, to live a holy life dedicated to Him. That night, instead of sleeping, I wrestled with excitement and anxiety over the magnitude of the moment soon approaching. We were one step closer to our dream of being parents.

If God Is With You, Who Can Be Against You?

Around 8:30 am the next morning, excited and anxious for our long-awaited moment to arrive, a terrible bang abruptly woke us up. It took us totally by surprise and put our nerves on edge. It was a deafening noise, unfamiliar to us, that left our ears ringing for some time, as if a bomb had gone off next to our bed. Frantically, I ran outside to the backyard in search of the origin of the explosion and to check on our dogs, while Ricardo looked through every room in the house.

While I was still outside, unaware of the danger lurking nearby, another blast went off, this time louder. It felt like it came from just a few yards away from where I was standing. If I was scared before, now I felt terrified. I ran back inside in search of Ricardo and found him standing in front of a window adjacent to our master bedroom staring at the floor. He pointed to debris scattered on the floor that appeared to be splintered wood and shattered metal and then turned to me with fear and shock in his eyes as he said, "Call 911. Someone is shooting at our house!"

In just minutes, that peaceful morning had turned into one of frantic chaos and nervous desperation, full of police officers and detectives asking dozens of questions in their search for motives and possible suspects. I recall that one of the agents, while examining the hole the bullet left behind in our window, commented to his partner how it most likely came from a high-caliber rifle. The bullet had come in through the window and impacted a metal support beam, which in turn caused it to veer away from our bed and into the connecting hallway. He said we were lucky. If not for the bullet hitting that beam, we could've been struck and possibly severely injured.

All this drama began to feel like a nightmare specifically designed by the enemy to deny, discourage, and ultimately destroy God's plan for our lives. But Ricardo and I weren't having it! Now more than ever we understood the dynamics going on behind the scenes, the battle being waged in the supernatural realm for the future of our marriage, our ministry, and our child. What God had in store for us was big enough to warrant an attack of this magnitude from Satan, but we were up for the challenge! We determined then and there not to let the events of that morning rattle us or shake our faith in God's plan for our day at the fertility clinic and, ultimately, our lives.

Little did we know that the situation was still unfolding. No sooner had we thought the worst had passed than another explosion went off. The house was still full of officers and detectives, and each one of them began to reach for their bulletproof vests and take cover wherever they could find it. It looked like a scene from an action movie—officers with guns drawn, spread out throughout our house, peeking out windows for any sign of the perpetrator, and us in the middle of it all.

Of course, we did what anyone in our situation would do. Ricardo and I threw ourselves on the kitchen floor and begin to pray for God's protection. We were short on bulletproof vests and didn't have guns to defend ourselves, but we knew God had angels fighting for us at every turn and a hedge of protection around our lives. That being said, I still couldn't believe out of all the days, all the hours, and the thousands of houses and windows in our area alone, this was happening to us on that day of all days, at the most crucial hour, in our house, and through our bedroom window. "What about our doctor's appointment?" I thought. There was no way to change it with such short notice. Plus, we had been planning and preparing for three whole months for the visit we had scheduled that morning. What about my emotional state and the calm I was emphatically prescribed? It was clearly gone.

In that moment, fearful, worried, and looking for answers, I glanced at Ricardo. He hugged me even stronger and said with a calm and reassuring voice, "Don't worry. Everything will be alright. This is, without a doubt, an attack from the enemy. But we know that He who is in us is stronger, and the outcome is already decided. We win!" Those words instilled peace in my heart and assured me that what we were doing not only had God's support but would be something miraculous and spectacular—so much so that it had the enemy fighting till the last minute with all he had in his arsenal to destroy it.

What seemed like hours passed, and then finally one of the detectives received a call informing him they had a suspect in custody that fit the description of the person they were looking for. He was found with a high-powered rifle in hand walking the golf course by our house. It turns out, this young man, under the effects of drugs, had stolen a rifle from an adjacent house whose owner happened to be a police officer. He then spent that morning firing at will into houses and at random people around the neighborhood.

It was clear to us that nothing that occurred that morning had been a coincidence. Instead, it was a perfectly timed and orchestrated attack by the enemy against all that God was planning for our lives. We also understood that luck didn't have anything to do with the bullet veering off the metal beam and sparing us from any physical hurt or, worse yet, death. It was all God's divine intervention! God had taken an event that had originally been planned as a way to discourage us and rob us of our dream and turned into a morning of affirmation and a double portion of His blessing, which would soon surpass our greatest expectations.

THE MOMENT ARRIVES

On our way to the doctor's office we couldn't help but thank God for His protection. It had been a morning contrary to everything the doctor had prescribed, but the last word was God's to have. As we arrived at the office, we decided not to share anything with the doctor for fear he would cancel the whole procedure. We walked in with confidence and faith, leaving everything that had occurred behind and embracing the peace that God had instilled in our hearts. The procedure was relatively quick, and in just a few hours I was sent home to rest.

The following weeks as we awaited the results of the treatment were full of joy, dreams, and wonder, mixed in with a bit of uncertainty. I would spend most of my time in the room my father had painted visualizing my baby and hearing her voice call out to me, "Mom." I reminisced about all those Mother's Days I had remained seated in church when they had called out to the youngest, the oldest, and those with the most children to come forward and receive their gifts. I pictured the many sympathetic looks I'd received throughout the years from friends, family, and people I didn't even know. And now here I was, waiting for my miracle to arrive. The percentages and statistics were not in my favor, but I had the Master of the impossible on my side, and that was more than enough.

July 27, 2009, was a day like any other. Ricardo and I were having lunch at a Mexican restaurant we regularly frequented. We were trying to forget the unforgettable, putting aside if only for a few minutes the anxiousness fueled by our high expectations. I had been visiting the doctor's office every week to give blood samples and had been hopeful they would soon call with the good news, but so far we had heard nothing. At the restaurant we placed our order, and when it arrived, we lifted a thankful prayer. But before we could take our first bite, the phone rang. It was an unknown number, but when I answered, a voice spoke out, "Congratulations, Susana. You're going to be a mom!" I was speechless. Could I be imaging what I just heard? I began to cry, and without a word, passed the phone to Ricardo. He, taken aback by my immediate reaction, responded and also heard those wondrous words: "Sorry to disturb you, Mr. Rodríguez. I'm only calling to inform you that everything was a success, and you guys are going to be parents! Your wife is pregnant!" Ricardo quickly thanked her and hung up. We looked at each other, and wiping tears from our eyes, left the restaurant with hearts overflowing with happiness.

I don't recall what we ordered that day or if we even paid the bill; all I remember is being on cloud nine. In that specific moment, for just an instant in our lives, the world as we knew it ceased to exist. Nothing else mattered—only that we were going to be parents. It was a day we would never forget. I couldn't stop thanking God for His goodness and mercy in our lives. After everything we'd lived through, our heavenly Father had leaned in to hear and extended His hand to bless, just like He had done with Hannah. Our miracle was on its way!

Now I, Susana Rodríguez, would have the opportunity to teach my son or daughter how to live a righteous life before God, and

Ricardo would have his reward and earthly legacy and a chance to show his child that true love and forgiveness can conquer anything. After sixteen years of ardent prayer and what for us seemed like endless patience, the moment had finally arrived.

God's timing is impeccable. He doesn't work according to our schedule but within a perfect and precise plan that He alone has the power to control. He knew when we would be ready for the blessing and how it should arrive. The waiting process was difficult, and we sometimes doubted and questioned the timing of it all, but looking back, we wouldn't change the order of a single thing, nor alter a fraction of a millisecond within His divine timeline.

A FINAL DECISION

My pregnancy was amazing. I didn't suffer from nausea at all, and that alone was reason enough to be overjoyed. I appreciated every instant, especially seeing my belly grow, which turned out to be one of the most moving experiences I've had in my life.

A few weeks after receiving the good news, we visited the doctor for a routine ultrasound. In the middle of the exam the nurse stopped and excused herself, exiting the room abruptly and leaving Ricardo and I wondering what was going on. She returned a few minutes later with another technician, which only added to our uneasiness, especially since they were both staring intensely at the ultrasound on the screen. Once again, they excused themselves. This time they returned with the IVF specialist, who in turn broke the news that changed everything: "Ricardo and Susana, you guys are expecting triplets!" What? We couldn't wrap our head around what the doctor was telling us. He told us there were three heartbeats and that I was pregnant with triplets. They left the room once more to consult with another specialist, leaving Ricardo and I in a state of shock.

Fear began to overwhelm my mind, and the tears started to flow. We definitely weren't ready to hear those words, and they left me paralyzed. Ricardo quickly assessed the situation and put his arms around me in an effort to ease my anxiety and comfort my heart. Again he said, "It's OK. Everything is under control. God will not give us more than we can manage, and I know He will supply all our needs, come what may." We gave thanks for those three little angels growing inside me and commended them to God's care.

The specialist returned, and my mother along with him. The doctor still had a few things to share with us that would put a damper on all our joy. He began explaining how difficult and strenuous it is for a woman to carry three babies and how improbable it would be for me to make it to full term given several factors, including the size of my uterus, my age, and the fact that it was my first pregnancy. That being said, he told us, any one of them—or possibly all of them—could be born with serious complications and most likely would have to deal with long-term issues throughout their lives. They could very well be children with special needs who would never have a chance at a normal and productive life.

Having presented all the possible negative scenarios associated with carrying three babies, including how they put even my own health in jeopardy, he gave us an impossible choice for a mother to make: something called selective reduction. He was asking me to make a devastating and heartbreaking choice: choose to end the life of baby A, B, or C to save the other two.

Once again, our character was put through the fire and our faith was being tested. Here we were being confronted with an impossible situation, facing insurmountable odds, and being told the ball was in our court. But there wasn't much to think about, nor any pause in our response. We would not be ending the life of any one of our babies. It was inconceivable to ask two people who had prayed so long and hard for this great opportunity to now put aside their emotions and ethical beliefs and discard the life of one of God's precious creations. The doctor pleaded with us to reconsider, offering us a week to think about it, still hoping for a change of heart. But in reality, there was nothing more to think about. God was in control. We began to pray, and depositing our fears and concerns at the feet of Christ, surrendered to His perfect will. We were willing to face whatever unknown the future held, but that decision would not be ours to make.

It was a difficult week to say the least, but we arrived back at the doctor's office ready to deal with whatever repercussions our decision would have. Although it was ultimately ours to make, the doctors were still gravely concerned for my health and what the final outcome would be. They did another ultrasound, but this time around they noticed one heartbeat weaker than the others. It was common, they said, but decided to run another test the next day. When I returned, the third heartbeat was no longer there. God had taken our baby back to heaven. An overwhelming sadness filled my heart, and on the way back home I couldn't stop crying.

I know that our baby was only a few weeks old and that I never held him in my arms, nor heard him call me mom, but in that moment it felt like a part of me had died. The pain was excruciating. I knew that God had worked according to His will, but from a mother's perspective, the loss was agonizing. To this day I wonder if that baby was a boy or girl, who he would have looked like, and how it would been to have him with us today. But with a thankful heart, I praise God and rest in the promise that I'll meet him one day.

A HAPPY PREGNANCY

Days became weeks, and weeks turned into months, and my belly—oh, my belly—began to grow in majestic fashion. I was well taken care of, though, by both my doctors and Ricardo alike, and they were months full of joy and contentment. For the first time in my life I felt fulfilled as a woman, and it showed. Everywhere I went, friends and strangers alike fussed over my belly, asking me when I was due and what I was having. With a great smile, I would take my time and detail the difficult process and long journey we endured to get to that point.

On the fifth month the moment of truth arrived: we had our highly anticipated gender reveal ultrasound. It was an exciting day, one that would alter our home and our destiny forever. Our babies would finally have a name! From the start, they had been showered with love and affection by their parents, Ricardo singing to them all the time and I having long conversations with them at all hours of the night, but we still didn't know their names!

The technician entered the room and began the process. He quickly confirmed the first one was a girl! Wow! I always dreamed of having a girl, of doing braids in her hair and dressing her like a princess. Now it would be a reality!

He continued checking, but before revealing the gender of baby number two he left the room, again putting us through a bit of unwanted stress and worry. A few minutes later, however, he walked in with a smile on his face to let us know baby number two was also a girl! Soon Madison and Miabella would arrive to fill our lives with happiness and joy!

Chapter 10

CALM IN THE STORM

by Ricardo and Susana Rodríguez

(**Ricardo**): After everything we lived through, our love had been transformed from an immature and superficial one to one of profound commitment and deep admiration. More than just husband and wife, we had now grown to be best friends. I recall after getting back together Susi and I always held hands wherever we went, and our newly acquired friends regularly pointed out how much they admired that particular romantic gesture in our relationship. They had no idea all we had suffered through while being apart and how valuable it was for us to feel each other's fingers intertwined and hands tightly gripped as we walked side by side through an ever more challenging world.

Although many years have passed, we've never forgotten the price we paid to be able hold hands again. Things we once took for granted are now precious and appreciated. Even today, whenever we go to the movies and the final credits start to roll, we have an unscripted routine of hugging each other before we walk out of the theater. I'm not sure when it started, but it's something that not only reinforces the love we have for one another but fills us with assurance and peace, knowing that after facing the worst, we're still together. Every day should be lived as if it were your last, and no loving gesture or word of affirmation should be left unexpressed or unsaid before your final breath. My father's death taught me that, and losing Susi reaffirmed it.

It didn't happen overnight, but over time and with great effort, the trust in our marriage returned, though it wasn't the same; no, it had grown to a level we never knew could be reached. It's difficult to explain, seeing as it was a divine transformation of the heart and mind, but the past was once and for all left behind. What once robbed me of my sleep and tormented my days no longer held me hostage, nor suppressed my ability to trust in Susi. We had developed a closer relationship, one that could only be attained by going through the fire together, by touching bottom and knowing we were not alone.

Now we were entering a new stage in our marriage, a different challenge that was no less demanding—being parents of twins. It was never part of our master plan, nor written in the script of our wildest dreams, but wow! What a blessing! When we finally came to terms that two little girls would soon be running around our house and into our hearts, we knew everything would change. Our priorities, plans, our trips, and even our ministry would have to take second place to the responsibilities of being parents.

But there was still a ways to go before they would arrive. Susi had a few more months of care and rest, and the doctors had warned us of the complications that could very well still lay ahead.

PREMATURE BIRTH

God continued being faithful to our lives. In those first months after we found out Susi was pregnant—and in ways that can only be explained as supernatural—He began to put everything in its place without much effort on our part.

Susi's pregnancy was mostly tranquil and uncomplicated, and although my commitments had me traveling constantly during the weekends, I tried hard never to miss a doctor's visit and to be home as much as possible. When they gave us the due date, I quickly cleared it in the calendar. I wasn't going to miss the birth of my daughters for anything in the world. They let us know it would be some time mid April, so I blocked off all those dates to assure I would be present for the greatest day of all.

At thirty-two weeks, Susi was feeling great and as happy as she could be, preparing every detail at home for the arrival of our girls and taking her now pretty substantial belly all over the place. But as those final weeks drew near, things took an unforeseen turn for the worse. One day, early in the morning, while partaking in one of the many childbirth classes she had signed up for, Susi began to feel ill. Her cousin Sara, who was also pregnant and attending the class, noticed what was happening and asked a nurse for help. They rushed her to the nearest triage, and after checking her vitals, gave her the unexpected news: she was going into premature labor. This, as you can imagine, sent Susi's mind running to a place of worry, thinking of the possible consequences and the grave situation that our girls would now have to confront. She was only thirty-two weeks pregnant, and our girls were too small yet to be born. The doctors admitted her right then and there, and she was put on bedrest with round-the-clock monitoring for the rest of her pregnancy.

The first thing we did while facing this surprising turn of events was to sound the alarm and put everyone on alert. Between our family and some close friends, we gathered together a team of intercessors and, trusting in God's promise, lifted Susi and our babies up in prayer and surrendered our worries and fears to the Lord. We knew He was in control. It seemed an immediate answer to prayer that after ten days of bedrest they sent her home with the condition that she continue staying off her feet and taking things slow.

I was incredibly grateful that the Lord allowed me to be home to support Susi on her transition home from the hospital. My schedule was extremely busy during that time, and it had me traveling all over the world. As I said, I had set aside the month of April to be home so I would be able to assist Susi in welcoming our girls into the world, but I was unprepared—in more ways than one—for

Susi to go into preterm labor at the end of January. The day she was released from the hospital, I was supposed to be in a concert. However, by what I now know was some divine intervention, there was a last-minute cancelation. Although I had repeatedly tried to reach the promoter to reconfirm all the details of the event, he never answered. This was rare and had me concerned at the time. The promoter had paid a deposit to secure the date, but he never followed up, nor communicated with our office. So, miraculously, I found myself being home with nothing to do except support Susi on that Saturday in February. On our drive home, I was so grateful God had it all planned out, but I had no idea just how significant a miracle the cancellation of that concert would be.

That same night, after having gone through those days of uncertainty and worry in the hospital and while resting comfortably at home, Susi's water broke. Once again, with fear and trepidation I gathered all her essentials, and we carefully made our way back to the hospital to face the unknown. As soon as we got checked in, the doctors rushed to our room and began working feverishly on buying some precious time for our babies. This lasted approximately twelve hours, but Susi's contractions were getting stronger with every passing minute, and there was only so much the doctors could do. Our girls were on the way.

Madison and Miabella were born at thirty-three and a half weeks on the sixth of February 2010, weighing exactly three pounds and twelve ounces each. They were small and fragile, but they were ours. It was an amazing and unforgettable day, and through it all we saw God's hand and favor over our lives and our baby girls'. I marveled at the way God had cleared my schedule so that I could be there, instead of at the concert. He knew Susi needed me there, that I needed to be there, and that the girls needed their father holding them as they took their first breaths and cried out for the world to hear. Even in the smallest of details, God was looking out for us for the sake of our emotions and well-being, and for our trust and faith in Him to grow.

I'll never forget Susi's reaction when she saw her little girls for the first time. The joy on her face, her beaming smile, and her thankful tears said it all. At last, after so many years of waiting, Susana Rodríguez was a mom. For myself, it was love at first sight. I couldn't believe I was the father of those two beautiful princesses. One look at their faces and I knew my life would never be the same. No longer would it be just Susi and I. Now, in an instant, we had become a family of four by the grace of God. There was so much more to live and fight for. In that moment we experienced a level of happiness that up until that point had eluded us.

Both girls spent seven weeks in the neonatal intensive care unit. They were each in their own private incubators, isolated from each other and us. They had all kinds of cables and tubes running from their tiny bodies, and they looked like extraterrestrials to those who saw them during that time. But they were ours, and they were beautiful.

The doctors would constantly remind us about the dangers Madison and Miabella were still facing at that a tender age and how long-term negative repercussions were still a big possibility. They mentioned possible issues with their eyesight, hearing, motor skills, and even asthma, since their lungs weren't fully developed yet. But those doctors didn't know who they were talking to. They had no idea what Susi and I had endured and overcome to arrive at that very place of fulfillment. Our faith had been tried, our character molded, and the assurance we had from God for the well-being of our daughters would not allow any of their words to undermine our resolute and positive attitude. Placing our trust in Him, we were more than confidant our daughters would be perfectly healthy.

I'd be lying, though, if I told you it was always easy. On the contrary, there were moments that tested our resolve. I remember one example in particular that really pushed us to the limits of our faith. One evening, the doctor, while doing his routine checkup on the girls, noticed Miabella was having serious health complications and required an emergency procedure to stabilize her condition. I was in Venezuela at the time on tour with Rene Gonzalez and Danny Berrios. That night, just before going on stage, I received a frantic call from Susi letting me know what was going on and asking for guidance as to whether or not we should proceed with the doctor's advice. Immediately we gathered together singers, musicians, and stage hands, and standing in front of the crowd, we lifted Miabella in prayer before the Lord, declaring healing over both her and Madison's fragile bodies and peace for Susi and myself, being so far from home.

God's hand was upon their lives, and after that night their progress was something only a miracle could explain. They left the hospital weighing five pounds each, one looking like mom and the other like me. We had two perfectly healthy girls, blessed and highly favored. As of the writing of this book they are eight years old and constantly ask us when we're going to be done publishing it, since we promised them a puppy when we were finished. That's our life now—one of promises and fulfillment, laughter and hugs, of great admiration and profound thankfulness. There aren't enough words in the dictionary to describe what Susi and I feel every time our daughters come in to our room, jump on our bed, and say with genuineness in their hearts, "Papi, Mami, I love you."

God Has a Plan and Will See It Through

God had all of this planned for us. Even after the mistakes we made, His purpose remained in place. But it was essential that repentance met forgiveness for all of it to be put it in motion. Forgiveness isn't easy; it requires courage in front of the naysayers, humility and patience above arrogance and pride, and a heart willing to leave the past behind and allow itself to be healed. In fact, if you don't allow your past to die, your future will never have a chance to live. I can assure you, God's way is the only way. Choosing to live in pursuit of His will and in obedience to His commands is the right decision and the only one that will allow you to finally attain the amazing life you've longed for and the freedom you so need. Forgiveness requires the embracing of love and mercy, even though justice and anger are knocking right outside your door. It's going against the statistics and percentages and sometimes feeling like you're one in a million, but you do it anyway. Forgiveness is irrational and unfamiliar to the human heart, but it's part of who God is and who we need to be.

I won't deny that the journey toward reconciliation is difficult and painful and that the storms of life will sometimes leave you weak and unwilling to proceed. But I can't say it enough—and even then my words fall short—that it's worth it! Never forget that God always allows the storms so they may bless your life, but that blessing is not found at the beginning of your struggle, nor in the middle; it is only when you reach the other side of that storm that the true nature of His plan is revealed. Even if the journey is agonizingly difficult, don't give up, for he who perseveres obtains the victory.

> *Blessed is the man who remains steadfast under trial, for when he has stood the test he will receive the crown of life, which God has promised to those who love him.*

> —JAMES 1:12, ESV

We all want to be promoted but not perfected, anointed but never tested; yet you can't have one without the other. There's a common phrase that pretty much describes the prerequisite to being used by God: No pain, no gain. In truth, no one ever says, "I'll take the narrowest, longest, and most difficult road please." We always look for the easiest, surest, and quickest way to reach our desired goals, avoiding life's deserts and storms whenever possible. But His Word is clear and unwavering, and everywhere we look we find examples of the significant price the great men and women of God had to pay to be used by Him. There is no easy way around this and no expediting process. If we want to be used in a powerful way, leaving our mark on this earth for His glory, there is a price to pay.

When we read in the Bible about the heroes of our faith, we have a tendency to skip through to the end to the see the magnificent results, disregarding in our haste the most important part, the middle. In the middle is where the process resides. A process is "a sequence of steps put together with a certain logic that focuses on reaching a specific result."[1] The result that God is looking for is to mold our character, increase our faith, and finally, bless our lives. If we are willing to trust Him to bring these results, we must also trust Him to guide us there according to His logic, not ours, and must remain faithful even when the path is challenging.

After embracing forgiveness and deciding to walk in obedience, Susi and I were immediately conscious of the fact that our decision to reconcile and fight for our marriage would take us down a solitary road, separating us from those who only focused on the sin that had been committed and the statistical impossibility of us making it work. Nonetheless, we felt in our hearts that our decision came with a great opportunity: the possibility of one day being used as instruments of hope and restoration in the lives of other couples. It was a ministerial promotion being offered to us—if only we were capable of making it to the other side of the desert of anguish, pain, humiliation, and shame and through the fire that burned and refined our hearts and minds, preparing us to be used by God one day. Praise God, we made it through. We were purified and perfected to be used by Him and have never been the same.

From the very moment when repentance met forgiveness, God began to plot our journey, a road that, having molded our character and strengthened our faith, has taken us to a more profound understanding of His power and greatness. Looking back, we see that period of isolation as a crucial part of God's divine plan for our lives, and we wear it like a badge of honor. We were separated by Him and for His glory! We've seen His blessing and favor, His provision and protection, and His glory manifested over our lives in more amazing ways than we can count. In fact, we have enough testimonies that we could easily write a few more books highlighting His faithfulness and mercy, His love and goodness, and His undeniable and always-present grace.

One instance in particular comes to mind that, without a doubt, placed God's power and mercy on full display. It happened while I was traveling outside of the US, and it changed our lives forever. After an amazing concert and an incredible night of ministering in which dozens of hearts surrendered to Jesus, I left my hotel in the early morning to catch the first flight back to Miami. It was 2:00 am on December 25, and I had promised my girls and Susi I'd be home by early Christmas morning to celebrate with them. The airport, though, was four hours away in another city, and getting there required traveling through precarious mountain terrain and dangerous weather conditions. I was driven by a young couple from the host church who were gracious enough to take the difficult journey and allow me to keep the promise I had made to my family. Before embarking on our trip, I spoke to Susi one last time, knowing I wouldn't have cell phone service to reach her while on the road. I'll never forget her last words to me: "Please put your seatbelt on." So I did.

We had driven the whole night and were approaching our destination just as the sun was coming up. But only a few miles away from the airport our worst fears became a reality: the driver, tired after having driven non-stop throughout the night, fell asleep, along with his wife, who was beside him in the passenger seat. He never slowed down as we hit the median, which in turn thrust us in the air, causing the car to roll over several times, finally coming to a halt wheels-up on the opposite side of one the most congested highways in the city.

Hanging from my seatbelt and in total shock, I tried to communicate with the couple in the front seat, but the husband was unconscious, and his wife was speechless. Even from the back seat I could see she was dealing with lacerations to her face and a possibly dislocated shoulder. I managed to release the seatbelt and, landing on the ceiling of the car, dragged myself out of one of the doors. Opening up the driver's side door, I helped the husband out, then his wife, and with the wheels of the car still spinning we walked to a safer location away from the center of the street.

It had all happened in an instant. We didn't have time to react, pray, or even say a single word. We stood there huddled together looking at the ensuing chaos of truckers, motorists, and curious bystanders walking around the mangled mess of what only a few minutes before had been a beautiful SUV. It was surreal and too much for anyone to make sense of, and all we could do we was hug each other and thank God.

As for me, there was not so much as a scratch on my body, and I didn't even lose my hat during the whole ordeal. I couldn't believe it! I should have been dead or severely injured, to say the least. God had, once again, spared my life.

> *For he will command his angels concerning you to*
> *guard you in all your ways.*
>
> —PSALM 91:11, NIV

After a few minutes, once the authorities had arrived and the couple was being attended to, I looked at my watch and saw there was still time for me to make my flight. So I said my good-byes, got in a taxi, and headed toward the airport. More than ever I wanted to be home.

Once at the airport I was able to communicate with Susi, but before I could tell her my harrowing story, she said to me, "The driver fell asleep, and you had an accident!" Did I hear correctly? How did she know? Could the news have traveled that far so quickly? She went on to tell me the that the Holy Spirit had woken her up that morning right around the time of the accident and overwhelmed her with the need to pray for me and the couple who had escorted me. Through prayer God revealed everything that would take place, but most importantly, He showed her that we would all be OK. It was incredible! From Susi reminding me to put on my seatbelt to her prayer for God's protection, God had His angels watching over me every step of the way!

Needless to say, Christmas was very special for the whole family that year. I arrived home while it was still morning to find Susi and the girls waiting for me at the door along with my mom, who had been informed of the accident and wanted to see for herself if I was OK. There were long embraces and thankful prayers, and in the end a wonderful time was had by all. But as I sat there watching my girls joyfully and innocently opening up their presents and singing Christmas carols when just a few hours earlier their dad had almost lost his life, I was profoundly moved by one thought: life is short and fleeting and can only truly be lived under the caring guidance and divine protection of a loving and almighty God. He carries us in the palm of His hand and will forever have the final word.

(Susana): God's promise to use Ricardo and I and all we experienced together has manifested itself over many years, both at home in Florida and around the world. Sometimes we witnessed it unfold in a direct and clear fashion within the parameters of our perfectly laid-out plans, and at other times it came as a totally sovereign act of God and well above our highest expectations. Since the beginning, Ricardo's songs and music ministry had always been the primary vehicle for our ministry, but in our hearts we always knew there was so much more we could offer and that the moment was quickly approaching when we would open up our lives and reveal the scars that for years we had so carefully tried to hide. Throughout the years we had shared very little about our testimony and the miracle of what God had done in our marriage, but He began to place in our paths couples who needed to hear what only we had to say. With words of hope and encouragement—and the healing power of the Holy Spirit—we helped them get back on track. Just like that, and without us even realizing what was happening at the time, God moved us into a new season of ministry, one that included the story of God's faithful hand over our relationship. I'd like to share one of those defining God moments that ultimately motivated us to write our story and reveal our scars.

OUR STORY REVEALED

We constantly receive invitations for concerts, conferences, special services, and other events that keep us exceedingly busy and transport us to all sorts of amazing and interesting places all over this beautiful world. A few years ago a call came into the office that wound up changing our perspective and ministerial focus. It was an invitation to minister in another country. Ricardo would have a concert on Saturday night and then share the Word on Sunday morning. The curious thing was that the pastor kept insisting that I too would travel with Ricardo. After having our daughters, I had tried to limit my trips considerably, especially when it required traveling to another country, so I was very hesitant at first to accept the invite. But the pastor wouldn't take no for an answer, and seeing as it was only two days, I grudgingly accepted.

After giving him the OK, the true motive behind the pastor's insistence that I travel with Ricardo came to light: he wanted *me* to preach! Immediately I told him no. I'm not a conference speaker, orator, or a pastor, and I was not comfortable standing in front of a congregation and speaking publicly. My Spanish wasn't good enough, I thought, and my nerves would be shot by the time I finished. I would happily accompany Ricardo, but speak to the congregation? Never!

A few weeks passed, and the pastor called again to confirm that everything was running smoothly on their end and to find out if I had changed my mind about sharing with the church. My answer remained the same. I told him apologetically, "I'm sorry, but no."

Meanwhile, the Holy Spirit had been tugging at my heart, and when I least expected it, He confronted me. It was true that I lacked the knowledge and experience of a seasoned speaker, but there was a story that needed to be told, and it was one that only I could share. Although my mouth kept saying, "Never," my mind was now thinking, "Maybe." In the end my heart placed the deciding vote and said yes. I spoke to Ricardo, and he, with a joyful grin, gave me his unconditional support.

Quickly, I began to study, reading the Bible and whatever study guides I could get my hands on to nourish my mind and strengthen my self-esteem. But I had decided to avoid talking about our marriage and prepare something more along the lines of God's love and faithfulness. I still didn't feel comfortable sharing about my failures and shortcomings in a public forum.

When we arrived in the city we were taken directly to the venue where the concert would be held, and as we entered through the doors we came to the realization that it was a couples banquet all along. The place was full, and everyone was sitting with their spouses at their assigned tables, dressed in their finest attire and awaiting the evening's concert. There was expectation in the air, but even with all the fanfare and regality of the night, there was something that didn't feel quite right, something that was seemingly being masked by superficial smiles and shallow conversation, though I couldn't put my finger on it. I was already reluctant and nervous about speaking, and having scouted the terrain, whatever little courage I had mustered on my way there was quickly disappearing.

Ricardo and I were led to our designated spots at a table with other couples, and we began to eat. There, surrounded by couples of all ages, I noticed a young lady with a sad complexion and a distant stare in her eyes. She was not eating. The pastor came by and introduced her as his wife, which only increased my uncertainty about speaking. I was extremely nervous, and inside I kept asking God to please change the program so that I wouldn't have to talk. Ricardo sang, and it was a great blessing for everyone there, but as the night was coming to an end the pastor leaned over to me and whispered, "Are you ready for tomorrow?" I wanted to scream, "No!" but I just nodded my head instead.

We arrived at the hotel, and with anxiousness in my heart and my stomach churning, I got on my knees and began to pray. I needed to feel Jesus by my side and God's strength sustaining me, because the fear I was battling against was terrifying. I had a very uneasy night going over my notes and everything I had prepared, but nothing seemed to be making any sense. Finally, after hours of getting nowhere and feeling frustrated, I surrendered to my sleep.

Early morning the next day, Ricardo, seeing the emotional state I found myself in, laid his hands on me and lifted up a prayer of faith and affirmation. His words were encouraging and filled me with peace, dissipating the anxiety that had inundated my heart. That calm that I so needed gave me clarity, and I told Ricardo that I felt God prompted me to discard the careful notes I had made and instead speak from the heart about our marriage, sharing our story instead. He was in agreement, and we left to go to the church.

When we arrived, it wasn't what I had imagined. Their building was under construction, so they were holding services under a massive tent adjacent to the building. I recall it was cold inside, caused partially by the strong mountain winds blowing through the tent and also because of the looks of the people in the church. The women were all serious, unfriendly, and kept their distance, and again I felt unprepared and out of my element. At a distance I could see the pastor's beautiful wife, still with a sad and lonely face, also looking out of place.

Ricardo ministered in worship, and as he sang there were several moments I wanted to tell him to keep singing and take his time. The fear I felt was debilitating. I was paralyzed by inadequacy and insecurity, which made me feel incapable of sharing in front the congregation, especially to people who seemed distant and unreceptive. But when the Holy Spirit goes before you and Jesus is by your side, victory is guaranteed. I knew He had called me to this moment, and it was time to take the next step in faith.

Therefore, when Ricardo introduced me, I put on the armor of Christ and walked forward with confidence. He handed me the microphone, and beneath that cold, windy tent, and in front of the seemingly even colder congregation, I began to open up my heart. I spoke about my infidelity and the damage it caused to our marriage and our lives. I shared about the consequences and the process, about forgiveness and mercy, and the total restoration that exists when there is genuine repentance and a complete abandoning of the ways of sin.

I was brief and didn't share details, but the result was immediate. All those present looked at me as if they had seen a ghost. Some even stood up and left. It was embarrassing and emotionally devastating, leaving me with the unique and profound desire of wanting the earth to open up and swallow me whole. I felt naked and judged by people I didn't even know. In the end, it was worse than I could have ever imagined. The only thing that surpassed that terrible drama was the reaction of the pastor. He was stepping out of the church when I first began to talk about my transgressions, but as soon as he heard the word *adultery*, he stopped in his tracks and looked me straight in the eyes. His demeanor changed, and his lifeless and somber expression gave me the inkling he was none too happy about the whole thing.

Perhaps you find yourself thinking, "What else could have gone wrong?" I'm glad you asked. During my talk, the winds began to blow. At first, it swept through in a soft and pleasant sort of way, occasionally blowing my hair back. Nothing too alarming. But then, the more I spoke about our testimony and shared the truth about sin and adultery and the power of repentance and forgiveness, the more the winds began to increase. The sand started to pelt my face, and it got so bad that at one point I truly thought we would all be blown away like a scene from *The Wizard of Oz*. It felt like something out of this world and very much supernatural. Ricardo came back up and finished with a song, making an altar call for couples who were struggling in their marriages. No one came forward.

THE PURPOSE IS REVEALED

When we arrived back at the hotel that afternoon, I threw myself on the bed and began to cry. I had opened up my heart and, with transparency, shared something so intimate and personal without any positive result whatsoever. I felt confused and defeated, and I questioned God about everything that had transpired that morning. Finally, I fell asleep, longing to be home as soon as possible and to get away from everyone and everything associated with that horrible trip.

A couple of hours later, Ricardo woke me up to let me know the pastor and his wife would be picking us up to have dinner later that night—plans I was not too happy about, as you can imagine. Nevertheless, I got dressed, and when they arrived we drove to a restaurant nearby where we had dinner and partook in polite conversation.

All the while, I kept questioning God about that fateful morning. "Why did You have to bring us to a faraway country simply to embarrass us?" I asked. "Why would You have us waste our time and allow us to open up our hearts to people who clearly didn't care about anything we had to say?" I wanted answers and clarity, but through it all, God remained patiently silent.

At the end of the dinner they asked if we wanted some coffee, to which we responded in the affirmative. They then proceeded to take us up a ski lift to a secluded coffeehouse at the top of the mountain. There we sat watching the snow fall as we drank our coffee.

Then suddenly, something totally unexpected happened. The pastor began to open up and share what was burdening his heart. He started off by letting us know how difficult it was for him to say what he was about to say. He told us he had been praying for God to show him someone who had gone through the same thing he and his wife were now going through and had made it to the other side victoriously. His wife had been unfaithful to him, and he was still dealing with the repercussions of that sin and the heartbreak and pain that it had caused. He added that although he had chosen to forgive his wife, the congregation hadn't shown the same type of mercy and grace. He asked many questions, wanting to know how we did it—how we managed to regain the trust and happiness in our marriage, how we overcame the shame associated with that type of sin, and how now we were able to walk together side by side, holding hands, without any symptoms whatsoever of that terribly profound wound.

It was clear he had, had no idea who he was inviting to his concert. He never imagined that God's plan had been set in motion way before he even made that first phone call to our office. He had insisted so much that I speak that Sunday, not knowing that what I was going to share were pages of his own life. In that moment Ricardo and I understood that it was all part of God's plan to use us as examples of His grace and forgiveness.

Almost instantly we noticed a drastic change in his complexion. He was more relaxed and even showed his smile. Meanwhile, his wife had begun to cry quietly. The pastor tried to console her, but the more he asked what was wrong, the heavier she wept. After a few minutes she composed herself and, with desperation in her voice, also opened up. She confessed, "I had planned to take my life in church today. I couldn't take any more of the rejection and contempt and all the judgmental looks of shame and disgust I've received from those around me. As I heard Susana's testimony I was reminded that I wasn't alone and that it is possible to start over. If you guys made it, I feel in my heart that with God's help we can too." She gave her husband the suicide note she had been carrying in her purse, and they hugged desperately.

My heart was overcome, and I also began to cry. In that moment everything became clear. God's purpose had been fulfilled. This beautiful couple had found the right place to look for an example of our heavenly Father's restoring power. I couldn't contain myself any longer, and walking outside into the snowy night, I began to talk to God. All I could do was thank Him over and over again and at the same time ask Him to forgive me for all the questions and doubts I carried with me throughout the whole trip. As I saw God's plan develop in such an inexplicable and amazing fashion, once again the words from that letter I read years before came to mind.

What a precious vessel you will be to me then. A vessel once humbled and hurt and then healed to be a healer.
This is my plan for you.

—GOD[2]

I had been healed to be a healer. I was the vessel that God was using! Me! The sinner who tried so many times to end her life; the one who couldn't sleep in her own bed because she didn't feel worthy; the scorned, forgotten, unqualified, and shunned. God had made something precious from the vile! Oh, how great is the love of God and how immense is His mercy!

That was the decisive moment that impressed in us the need to write this book—to share with transparency and sincerity an intimate story of shame and suffering that has probably made you feel uncomfortable and confronted you in more ways than one. But Ricardo and I are in one accord with this belief: if just one person is moved to forgive, if simply one broken heart finds healing through mercy, and if our lives need to be exposed as examples of restoration for all of it to be possible, then it has literally been worth the embarrassment to write it.

Ricardo and I have learned a lot since that experience. We have embraced our testimony as the jumping-off point for the ministry God has given us, and we are beyond grateful we get to reach people at this vulnerable and pivotal place in their walk with God and their spouse. Our own story taught us about the power of meeting repentance with forgiveness—in all cases, but especially in the case of infidelity—but our time ministering to other families broken by sin has made this truth crystal clear: wherever your choices have brought you, wherever others' choices have impacted your life in a way that caused wounds instead of healing, there is a way back. Healing is possible, both for you and for the broken relationship that lay in front of you. You are not stuck where you are today.

God is a God of healing and restoration. There is no wound so deep that He cannot heal it. There is no heart so broken that He cannot put it back together. There is no relationship so fractured that He cannot repair it and make it stronger than ever before. If our story is not enough to give you hope, consider the Book of Hosea. In that book, we read about how God used a marriage broken by infidelity to demonstrate the depth of His love and the lengths to which He would go to repair His relationship with us. If God could heal and restore the marriage of Hosea and Gomer, we know He can do it for you.

If as you read this book you empathized with Susi's part of our story—perhaps you have been unfaithful to your spouse, or maybe you have been feeling unfulfilled in your marriage—we want you to know that you are loved and precious to the God who knit you together in your mother's womb and sent His only Son to die so that He could know you. If you have not yet repented of your sin, stop what you're doing, and surrender your heart and life back to Him now. Make the decision not to continue those actions but instead to earnestly pursue holiness and wholeness. Confess your actions to your spouse, and commit to rebuilding the relationship and the hearts broken by unfaithfulness. If you have repented, remain steadfast in your pursuit of God. Seek Him first, and follow His leading as you intercede for your spouse and your marriage.

If you are reading this and identify with Ricardo's role in our testimony, it is time to cling to the Word of the Lord and seek His face and His counsel. It takes the unconditional grace and mercy that only comes from a heart filled with the love of the Father to be able to extend forgiveness, receive healing, and walk forward into your future, individually and with your spouse. Do not try to make that journey on your own. Abide in the Lord and remain willing to accept that your spouse may not be the only one who needs to make changes in his or her life and character.

We hold no bitterness or resentment at all to those who, possibly because of their naive and immature perception of God's heart or their own unhealed wounds and unprocessed emotions, could not grant us the support we needed during our moment of despair. After all, it's impossible, after being recipients of so much love and forgiveness and after living under the incomparable grace of God, to look at anyone with judgment and contempt. Nonetheless, we are sure to steer others walking a similar path to be sure to choose their own friends and counselors with greater care than we did. We recommend you seek the help and support of a trusted friend, pastor, or counselor who will intercede for you in prayer and who shares your passion for seeing God reconcile your relationship with your spouse.

It's very possible that the reason you've read our story is because in your heart you too desire to begin again, to start anew, leaving the past behind with all of its failures, burdens, and painful memories. It could be that in this very moment you're standing in the epicenter of the most difficult storm of your life, and no matter how hard you've tried, you simply can't find a way out. We pray the message in our book has been clear and direct and you've understood that Jesus offers you victory through surrender, freedom through forgiveness, and hope through obedience. The past will never be set right; it can only be surrendered. The chains of resentment and bitterness will not dissolve with time; they can only be broken with forgiveness. And the dreams that were shattered will not miraculously reappear, but they can be remade and reshaped to surpass even your wildest expectations if you're willing to obey God's will for your life. If you are, repeat this prayer with us:

Jesus, I surrender my life and my will to You. Take me as the broken vessel I am, and as the potter molds the clay, make me new. My marriage is Yours, my dreams are Yours, but above all, my heart is Yours. Help me to forgive those who have trespassed against me and teach me to forgive myself as You have forgiven me. Heal the wounds of our pasts and restore the hope for our future. I declare victory over my marriage, and that which You have united, let no enemy separate. In Your precious name I pray. Amen!

It is our profound desire that, in sharing our story, those who read it find within its pages hope in their darkest hour, courage to forgive, and if you're a leader, the willingness to always offer both. That decision could save both lives and marriages.

Remember, love conquers all, forgiveness has no limits, and faith can move mountains!

NOTES

CHAPTER 1: A LOVE STORY REVEALED

1. National Parents Organization, https://www.nationalparentsorganization. org/blog/3924-psychotherapist-st-3924 (accessed June 2, 2016).

CHAPTER 4: GOD IS FAITHFUL

1. Quote by D. L. Moody accessed at Cheryl Lavin, "Character is what you are in the dark," Chicago Tribune, March 18, 1990, available at http://articles. chicagotribune.com/1990-03-18/features/9001230543_1_character-treats-index (accessed May 12, 2018).

2. Rick Warren, *Liderazgo con propósito* [Purpose Driven Leadership] (Miami, FL: Editorial Vida, 2008), 10.

CHAPTER 5: BROKENNESS AND ANOINTING

1. David Augsburger, *Perdonar para ser libre* [*Freedom of Forgiveness*] (Grand Rapids, MI: Editorial Portavoz, 1977), 21.

2. Ibid, 19.

CHAPTER 6: RETURN TO ME

1. Claire Cloninger, *Postcards for People Who Hurt* (Dallas, TX: Word Publishing, 1995), 107.

CHAPTER 10: CALM IN THE STORM

1. Definition, s.v. "process," http://definicion.mx/proceso/ (accessed July 21, 2016).

2. Claire Cloninger, *Postcards For People Who Hurt*, 107.

ABOUT THE AUTHORS

Ricardo and Susana have shared 25 years of marriage and over 20 years in music ministry. Together they have impacted millions of lives across this planet with songs of hope and faith and a testimony that demonstrates the healing and restorative power of our heavenly Father. They are the parents of a set of beautiful twins, Madison and Miabella, who are now eight years old.

Ricardo has received numerous awards and nominations for his 17 recording projects, among them: *Alabanzas del Pueblo* ("Praises From the People") Series (1999–2001), *Sinceramente Ricardo* ("Sincerely Ricardo," 2005), *Eso Es* ("This Is It," 2008), *Calma* ("Calm," 2011), and *Huele a Lluvia* ("Smells Like Rain," 2015).

With their debut book in Spanish, *¿Y Si Comenzamos de Nuevo?* (2016), they embarked on a new stage in their ministry— as authors. In this autobiographical work, they share with honesty and transparency what happens when repentance meets forgiveness. It is the testimony of their failures, triumphs, process, and, ultimately, God's faithfulness. Their lives are an example of what our God is capable of doing with hearts that are passionate and surrendered to Him.

The Rodrígueze's family is a member of Jesus Worship Center, which is pastored by Frank and Zayda López, in the city of Miami, Florida.

For more information on Susana & Ricardo's ministry, please visit our website at:
www.whatifwestartover.com
www.ricardorodriguez.com
Facebook: What If We Start Over
Facebook: RicardoRodriguezAlaba
Twitter: Ricardoalaba
Instagram: RicardoRodriguezOficial
Instagram: susanarodriguezmin

For information on booking Ricardo & Susana, and/or purchasing their book for your ministry or church please call (305) 256-2556 or email: whatifwestartover@gmail.com.

Starting Over Ministries
PO Box 565878
Miami, FL 33256